# *Introduction to*
# SERVICE
*What It Is and What It Should Be*

# *Introduction to* SERVICE

*What It Is and What It Should Be*

# Harry Katzan Jr.

# INTRODUCTION TO SERVICE
## WHAT IT IS AND WHAT IT SHOULD BE

*iUniverse books may be ordered through booksellers or by contacting:*

*iUniverse*
*1663 Liberty Drive*
*Bloomington, IN 47403*
*www.iuniverse.com*
*1-800-Authors (1-800-288-4677)*

*ISBN: 978-1-5320-3596-8 (sc)*
*ISBN: 978-1-5320-3598-2 (hc)*
*ISBN: 978-1-5320-3597-5 (e)*

*Library of Congress Control Number: 2017916278*

*Print information available on the last page.*

*iUniverse rev. date: 10/28/2017*

*To Margaret, as always*

# Contents

# PREFACE

Service is a subject we should all know about, because it is the up and coming discipline for the 21st century. This book covers what a service is and what it should be. In ordinary everyday language, a service is an activity that one entity provides for another entity, such as auto repair or dental work. The entity performing the service is called the service provider and the entity receiving the service is called the service consumer, even though different names usually apply. Services are important to people in business, government, education, health care and management, religion, military, scientific research, engineering, and other endeavors that are too numerous to mention. The subject is important to providers and consumers of services, alike. In fact, most service providers – be they individuals, businesses, governments, and so forth – are also consumers of services during the course of everyday life. A sage has said that in reality, everything is a service, because a consumer – when receiving an activity of some sort - is actually providing a service to the provider. Think about it. Even a person with an MD degree is actually not a service provider unless he or she has patients. This is a subject for another chapter or even another book.

Today, most of us are employed in performing a service of some kind. Typical examples are doctors, dentists, lawyers, teachers, entertainers, news people, dry cleaners, and maintenance workers. Actually, this should not be a surprise, since much of what we do in everyday life involves using a service. A service activity is characterized by the fact that the result is usually intangible, meaning, in this instance, that an artifact of some sort is not produced as a result of the service experience, as in the manufacture of a product. Most people never think about the many aspects of a service engagement. Therefore, basic concepts and some service definitions are definitely in order.

A *service* is a client/provider interaction that creates and captures value for both participants, and a *service system* is a system of people and technology that adapts to the changing value of knowledge in the system. The study of service is actually the study of service systems.

To be more specific, a *service system* is a socially constructed collection of service events in which participants exchange beneficial actions through a knowledge-based strategy that captures value from a provider-client relationship. The inherent service strategy is a dynamic process that orchestrates or coordinates components, employees, partners, and clients in the co-production of value. Based on a theoretical framework for creating economies of coordination, research on service incorporates a microanalysis of various and diverse service events, so as to develop a view of the services landscape.

The study of service is an abstraction of service systems in the same way that the study of computers is an abstraction of computer-based information systems. The procedure, in both cases, is to take a piece of an existing system and put it under the microscope of academic scrutiny. In this particular instance, we are taking a service centric view of organized systems, where traditional organizational functions are candidates for being packaged as well-defined services.

This book is an introduction to service for employees, managers, and other persons involved in business, education, and government.

Chapter one, entitled *Services*, is the key chapter. It is easy to read and totally accessible to all readers. It sets the framework for the rest of the book and would be useful for persons from all walks of life. Essentially, chapter one covers what services are.

Chapter two, entitled *Systems*, describes services as a collection of resources and economic entities, capable of engaging in or supporting one or more service events. The resources are the infrastructure and other facilities necessary to support the service process. The economic entities are the service provider and service client that co-produce the service event. In the case of possession processing services, the service environment consists of one or more tangible objects that serve as the service object of a service process. In this sense, the service object is referred to as the *"operand"* of the service process and denotes just who receives the service. In most cases, a larger service system is required to sustain a service event.

Chapter three, entitled *Information*, describes how information and communications technology (ICT) has enhanced how we live and work. An *information service* is a resource capable of supporting a service event or instantiating a service event based on information. In other words, an information service can assist in the execution of a service, such as in retailing, or it can actually be the service as when buying a pair of shoes on the Internet or looking up something on the World Wide Web. The resource is a service provider that can take the form of a person or a computer. The execution of an information service event requires a service client that can also take the form of a person or computer such that the provider and client must interact in order to co-produce the service.

Chapter four, entitled *Management*, moves the subject of services into the realm of management. Through the application of information and communications technology (ICT), many organizations have encapsulated everyday operations enabling them to go through a transformational process to achieve revenue growth by being able to respond more quickly to changing market conditions and by being more effective and efficient in the application of services. This chapter describes modern services management.

Chapter five, entitled *Business*, completes the structure of the discipline of service. This is an eclectic chapter that relates service to the worlds of business, education, and government.

Thanks to Margaret Katzan for helping with the manuscript.

HARRY KATZAN, JR.
*Hilton Head Island*

# 1

## A BRIEF LOOK AT SERVICE

The subject of service is the up and coming discipline for the 21$^{st}$ century. In fact, service encompasses technology, entrepreneurship, business growth, and innovation – four subjects that are of interest to most organizations. Service is important to people in business, government, education, health care and management, religion, military, scientific research, engineering, and other endeavors that are too numerous to mention. The subject is of interest to providers and consumers of service, alike. In fact, most service providers – be they individuals, businesses, governments, and so forth – are also consumers of service.

### Service and Employment

Today, most of us are employed in service. Typical examples are doctors, dentists, lawyers, teachers, entertainers, news people, dry cleaners, and maintenance workers. Actually, this should not be a surprise, since much of what we do in everyday life involves using a service of one form or another. Service activity is characterized by the fact that the result is usually intangible, meaning in this case that an artifact of some sort or another is not produced as a result of the service experience, as it is in the manufacture of products.

Most of us want to do better – in our jobs, education, business, professions, and so forth, and when we purchase services, it is really important that we get the best service for our time and money. But without a clear understanding of exactly what it is that constitutes a service, what differentiates one service from another, and how services operate and interoperate, continuous improvement will be a never-ending process of trial and error.

## Service Characteristics

The concept of service has its roots in economic activities that are classified as extractive, secondary, and services. *Extractive* refers to agriculture, mining, forestry, fishing, and so forth. *Secondary* refers to manufacturing and processing. *Services* refer to everything else, usually subdivided into domestic, trade and commerce, information services, and personal. This is a very general definition intended for the reporting by the government of economic conditions. In order to get a handle on services, we need a better definition.

A *service* is a provider/client interaction that creates and captures value. A unique characteristic of services, unlike agriculture and manufacturing, is that both parties participate in the transaction, and in the process, both capture value. In a sense, the provider and the client co-produce the service event, because one can't do without the other. It stands to reason that the roles of the client and the provider are different. In a doctor/patient service event, for example, the physician brings knowledge, time, and the necessary infrastructure. The patient brings himself or herself, a medical history, and a perceived situation that requires attention. During the service process, the participants exchange information in various forms, resulting in a change to the persons involved. The doctor's experience level and assets change, as do the patient's information level and physical or mental condition. There is more to it, of course, but this is the basic idea.

## Service and Organizations

In business, the case is slightly different. Some companies, such as professional firms, are totally service oriented. Other service companies, such as airlines and restaurants, have more complicated arrangements. An airline company, for example, could contract out its telephone reservation service to another company, perhaps in another country, called *outsourcing*. In this scenario, agreements, specifying responsibilities and expectations, are required in most cases, to guarantee a given level of service to the airline's customers. The same holds true for computer online services.

In government, services are governed by convention and law. Constituents use governmental resources for information and a variety of physical services. In many cases, it is difficult to tell who is providing the service and who is receiving it.

In education, the provider/client relationship can be complicated. Who is the provider and who is the client? Let's assume that the teacher provides the service to the student, by giving lectures and managing classroom activity. But it could be more complicated than that. Consider a university setting. Does the professor provide a service to the administration by teaching courses and doing the myriad of other things faculty do? But then again, one could look at it the other way around by contending that the purpose of the administration is to provide the educational infrastructure. So the teacher could be a provider of services and a client of services, at the same time. We will take a look at complex service arrangements in follow-on sections to this chapter and in later chapters.

Returning to the airline example, let's assume that an agreement is made with a company in another country to run a call center whereby passengers can make reservations and obtain information. Ostensibly, the objective of the airline is to save money, improve the bottom line, and help the top management look good to the shareholders. The airline is the client and the call center company is the provider. How does the client (that is the airline company, in this case), who is a stakeholder with something to gain or lose, effectively control the situation? They collectively draw up a *service level agreement* that governs the quality of service, the number of calls to be handled in a specified period of time, the duration of the agreement, and the costs involved. Why don't the patient and the doctor have a service level agreement? They do, but it is implicit in the social setting in which medical services are performed.

There is another twist to the airline example. Where do you and I – the passengers – fit in? Again, the call center operator provides an airline-related service to us and we are the clients, even though we are, in fact, the provider of the financial resources that make the whole process work. The call center company effectively has two clients: the airline at the macro level and the set of passengers at the micro level.

It is commonplace for services to exist at two or more levels, as demonstrated by the airline example, in a service arrangement called a *service package.* In a service package, services are performed at differing levels and the service level agreement must reflect that eventuality. When a collection of service processes exist and they are all performed at the same level, it is called a *service bundle.* So if you go to a medical facility comprised of a team of doctors that essentially performs the same kinds of things, the set of service events is called a service bundle. It follows in the case of the airline, that the service package contains a service bundle consisting of a group of telephone operators that provide services to passengers.

## Business Service

Some firms further complicate the picture by essentially being in two related service businesses at the same time. Consider an information technology (IT) company that provides services in two forms: consulting and outsourcing. With consulting, the firm tells a client how to do something, and with outsourcing, the firm does it for the client. As an example, the IT firm could advise as to what information systems the client needs and then develop those systems. Similarly, it could provide information on how to set up an IT operation and then run that shop after it is set up.

Related to IT services is a general class of activities known as *business services*. With business services, like IT services, there are two options: consulting and outsourcing. With business service consulting, organizations are advised about business functions, such as customer relationship management (CRM) and enterprise resource planning (ERP). Then, with outsourcing, the business services firm does it for you – perhaps in the areas of finance and accounting.

What we have at this point are multiple organizations, collections of people, and technology connected by value propositions and shared information, operating as a service system. More specifically, a *service system* is defined as a configuration of people and technology connected to another system of people and technology in order to co-create value for both organizations.

## Differences between Products and Services

It is useful to consider the differences between products and services. Products are tangible and services are intangible. Now that is a pretty general statement. An automobile, a garment, a table, and even a fast-food hamburger are examples of products. A doctor's visit, swimming pool cleaning, and package delivery are examples of services. On the surface, one could conclude that products are produced through some relevant sequence of operations, but that is not a defining characteristic, since most services also go through a sequence of steps. A product is an artifact – something you can see or touch. Clearly, the result of a service is something worthwhile – otherwise, why engage in it – but the result is a change in a person or possession, not in the creation of something.

Products are storable; services are non-storable. You can store any of the examples of products, given above. If you have your car cleaned or your lawn mowed, you can't exactly save that service. When a service is finished, it is done forever. Perhaps, a record of the service is archived, explicitly or implicitly, but once the stop button is pushed, that service machine is off. If a service has to be repeated, then it is another service event.

Another related difference is that services are generally regarded as perishable. The implication here is that if a seat on an airline flight is not used, then the value of that opportunity is lost. There are many parallels between services and events in everyday life. If you buy a fresh banana and don't eat it within a reasonable time period, its value is lost. You can buy another, but again, that is a different thing.

With products, consumption follows production. In fact, the build-store-sell and the sell-build-ship business models apply here. The build-store-sell model is usually related to commodities, such as toothpaste and school supplies. The sell-build-ship model is typically associated with larger items, such as computers, airplanes, and cruise ships. With services, consumption and production occur at the same time. This characteristic is related to the difference between product quality and service quality. With products, a quality assessment can be made before the customer enters the scene. With services, the client's view of quality is determined during the service process.

As product classes mature, they become standardized and competition shifts to price. Services are almost always customized. In general, product development is capital intensive, and the delivery of services is labor intensive.

It is important to recognize, however, that the creation of products may include services in the production process, and that services may also accompany production in the form of follow-on activity.

## Classification of Services

Given that services are pervasive in modern economies, there would appear to be so much diversity between them that it would be impossible to make any sense of the subject. After all, there does not seem to be much similarity between a lawn mowing operation and a service package for an airline – as simple examples. On the other hand, there has to be a set of common denominators that we could use to classify services so that we could draw some conclusions about organization, performance, and quality. After all, most of us would agree that clients would like to get the most for their money and, providers would like to receive the greatest return on their investment of knowledge, time, and effort.

Services are generally classified by at least five criteria, although one major criterion dominates. The minor factors are:

- degree of provider labor intensity
- degree of customer interaction
- level of provider knowledge
- amount of required client information

They are quantitative measures brought to a service event. The major factor is a qualitative attribute known as "service nature," consisting of a service object and a service result. We will also identify other factors in the second chapter and refine the material given here when we establish a complete set of comprehensive service models. Under consideration are the following candidates:

- a person
- a possession
- information

The service object is significant because it reflects that upon which a service is performed. In a previous section, we covered the subject of distinguishing services from goods. The service object is useful for distinguishing between services, and it preserves the roles of the provider and the client. In a generic sense, the provider does the work and the client pays for it, and the question of who or what gets the service is the determining factor in exactly how much of the other four quantitative criteria are applied to a particular service event.

### People Processing Services

In people processing services, the provider performs corporeal actions to the client. The client is part of the service production process and remains in the domain of the provider during the entire time of service delivery. There is simultaneity of production with consumption in a people processing service event, and the provider and client, are regarded as co-producing the service. A trip to the dentist typifies this type of service, as does a reservation made through an airline call center. A people processing service can change either the physical state of a person, the mental state of a person, or both. The physical state is something like increased fitness, manicured finger nails, or the location of a person. The mental state deals with non-physical attributes, such as increased knowledge, mental capability, or mental agility. Many people processing services perform both physical and non-physical benefits, as in medical services and sports coaching.

### Possession Processing Services

In possession processing services, the provider changes the state of one or more tangible objects under the jurisdiction of the client. Many possession processing services are straightforward, as in car washing and other maintenance activities. These services relate to the condition of an object and are regarded as physical services. Clearly, there are other attributes of service objects and one of the most common is ownership that puts retailing into the domain of service processing. In fact, some manufacturing operations consist of a sequence of services applied to a physical object or system. Another physical attribute is location, and an operation that provides components to a just-in-time production process is a form of service.

### *Information Processing Services*

Information processing services deal with the collection, manipulation, interpretation, and transmission of data to create value for the client. Accounting, banking, consulting, education, insurance, legal, and news are commonly experienced examples of information processing services. There are important issues with information processing services, such as representation (as with lawyers and accountants), infrastructure (as with computers, databases, and the Internet), and self service (as with online facilities, ATM machines, and other administrative functions). This type of service is covered in a separate chapter, later in the book.

## Characteristics of Services

In spite of the prevalence of services in everyday life, the subject is rarely considered and seldom defined. In business, services are commonly referred to as the non-material equivalent of a good. Services can be sold, purchased, and scheduled. To many people, a service represents something they cannot do themselves or do not want to do, or perhaps more importantly, something that can be done more efficiently or in a less costly manner by a specialized business entity. This is a recursive definition of a service system that would support the following modalities of service operation:

- tell me
- show me

- help me
- do it for me

In fact, the agricultural and manufacturing sectors of the economy employ services, and the services themselves often use services. That said, exactly what constitutes a service is still up in the air, and a summary of the major definitive characteristics is certainly needed.

*A service is a process.* This notion is paramount to recognizing the far-reaching importance of service as an academic discipline. A service takes input and produces output. In between the input and the output, there exist one or more steps that constitute the service process. Consider a simple medical example. A patient – the client – perceives a situation that requires attention. A contact with a medical provider is made and an appointment is scheduled for a service event. In general, the following three items of information are brought to the service process: the patient per se, a medical history, and the relevant information for the current problem. This is the client/customer input required for a service process. The physician performs the requisite consultation, diagnosis, and resolution that collectively constitute the service process. The output then consists of the diagnosis, prescription, prognosis, and update of the medical records. Additionally, the personal knowledge bases of the patient and physician are enhanced as a result of the service event.

*A service is heterogeneous.* This characteristic reflects the fact that each client/provider interaction in the form of a service event is unique. Some researchers refer to this characteristic as the fact that services are customized, either by design or by happenstance. Each service query to an information system or each instance of personal service, for example, is inherently different.

*A service captures value.* A service event creates a benefit to both the client and the provider, in the form of a change of state that is reflected in their physical condition or location, a change in their possessions, or in their assets. A service provider brings one or more of the following elements to the table: specific knowledge of the problem and solution domains, the time necessary to perform the service event, the physical wherewithal to perform the service event, and the requisite tools and equipment to perform the service event. Note that a location or infrastructure is not required since it may be associated with the client. The client provides the service object (i.e., the object or entity to which the service is applied) and necessary information, as required. The provider captures value through the execution of the service process. The client captures value as a result of the service process.

*A service cannot be inventoried.* The notion of opportunity loss is fundamental to service. An empty seat on an airline flight cannot be resold. We are referring to the service process and not the seat per se. The value lost to a service provider due to a missed appointment cannot be regained. This characteristic gives a time dimension to services. Clearly, there are other flights and other appointments, but the time assigned to the execution of a service process is lost forever once the service window has closed. Thus, a service capacity is said to be *perishable*, referring to the fact that it is "eliminated" when unused.

*A service is intangible.* Although this characteristic was alluded to above, it deserves special attention because the definition of service by the government uses the notion of a "change in the condition of a person or object" as the basis for classification. Services, especially in the areas of education and government, often result in social goods that are expressed in economic terms as hidden costs or opportunity costs.

*A service is consumed at the point of production.* This characteristic adds specificity to the recognition that a service is a process, even though it may be summarized for descriptive purposes as a service event. When a service terminates, it is finished. After the final step in a service process, the event is archived along with the consequent change of states of the client and provider.

*A service cannot be resold or given away.* It is not possible to pass a service on to another economic entity. The result of a service event is unique to that event, although information gained during the service process could theoretically be used by another entity. However, information resulting from a service event is not the same as the service event, because of the consumption characteristic. It's the process that counts. If your airline seat or dentist appointment is given to another person, then another service is materialized.

*A service is co-produced.* This characteristic emphasizes the fact that because of the simultaneity of client and provider participation and the fact that a service event does not result in the production of a good, but rather in the state of something, it is commonly referred to as the co-production of value in the sense that if either of the participants were not present for the service event, it could not be interpreted as being a service.

## Quick Summary

1. The subject of service is important to most people because they are employed in service and are also consumers of service. In the year 2000, U.S. service employment comprised 80% of the workforce. Surprisingly, very little attention is given to the service sector, in spite of the fact that most of us work in it.

2. A *service* is a provider/client interaction that creates and captures value. A unique characteristic of service, unlike agriculture and manufacturing, is that both parties participate in the transaction, and in the process, both capture value. In a sense, the provider and the client co-produce the service event, because one can't do without the other.

3. A service is generally classified by at least five criteria, although one criterion dominates. The minor factors are degree of provider labor intensity, degree of customer interaction, level of provider knowledge, and the amount of

client information, that are quantitative measures brought to a service event. The major factor is a qualitative attribute known as "service nature," consisting of a service object and a service result. The focus is on the service object in this chapter, because it reflects whether a service is performed on a person, a possession, or information.

4. There are several definitive characteristics of services. They are summarized as follows. A service is a process. A service is heterogeneous. A service captures value. A service cannot be inventoried. A service is intangible. A service is consumed at the point of production. A service cannot be resold or given away. And finally, a service is co-produced.

## Key Terms

The reader should be familiar with the following terms in the context in which they were used in the chapter.

| | |
|---|---|
| Client | Possession processing |
| Co-production | Processing |
| Heterogeneous | Provider |
| Information processing | Service bundle |
| Intangible | Service |
| Inventoried | Service package |
| Non-storable | Value proposition |
| People processing | |

## Selected Reading

Friedman, T. (2006). *The World is Flat: A Brief History of the Twenty-First Century*, New York: Farrar, Straus and Giraux.

Harvard Business Review, (1999) *Business Value of IT*, Boston: Harvard Business School Press.

IBM Almaden Services Research, (2006). "SSME: What are services?" http://almaden.ibm.com/ssme, 2006.

Katzan, H., (2008). *Service Science: Concepts, Technology, Management*, New York: iUniverse, Inc.

Maglio, P. and Zysman, J. (2007). *Toward a Science of Service Systems*, Sofcon 2007, Carnegie Mellon University, pp. 5-6.

Malone, T. (2004). *The Future of Work*, Boston: Harvard Business School Press, 2004.

Sampson, S. and Froehle, C. (2006). "Foundations and Implications of a Proposed Unified Services Theory," *Production and Operations Management*, Vol. 15, No. 2, pp. 329-343.

# 2

## SERVICE SYSTEMS

A *service system* is a collection of resources and economic entities, capable of engaging in or supporting one or more service events. The resources are the infrastructure and other facilities necessary to support the service process. The parties that stand to benefit from the service are the service provider and service client that co-produce the service event. In the case of possession processing services, the service environment would also consist of one or more tangible objects that serve as the service object of the service process. The service object is referred to as the *operand* of the service process. In this instance, the service target could be the client, a possession of the client, or an individual or an organizational entity over which the client has responsibility. In most cases, a service system is required to sustain a service event.

### Service Facilities

If a service provider and client can co-produce a service event, there must be some degree of geographical locality to the situation, in the sense that the client travels to the provider or the provider travels to the client or the client and provider execute the service event in a third-party location or they communicate via some form of interactive device and its corresponding media. In other words, the provider and the client have to get together.

### *The Service Factory*

The first instance is the case where the customer travels to facilities associated with the provider, such as an airline terminal, hospital, provider's office, restaurant, retail establishment, or hotel – to name only a few examples. Furthermore, let's refer to the provider facilities as the *service factory. The basic idea is that the customer remains at the service factory during service delivery.*

The situation quickly gets complicated because it depends on whether or not the service is associated with a tangible object, an intangible object, or a production supply chain. A *pure service* is a service not associated with tangible objects, such as in medical treatment, hair coloring, and personal transportation. The service event is scheduled, initiated, terminated, and archived – all in the service factory. In other words, the service is consumed in the service factory. Many service processes are comprised of several steps called the *service chain*. Other services, not just pure services, consist of a service chain, but this characteristic is normally associated with pure services. When a service process consists of a service chain, it is said to be "scripted," meaning that all clients essentially follow the same process. Clearly, a service script may be implicit in the service, such as a doctor's visit, or it may be explicitly prescribed as part of a formal service agreement. Depending upon the complexity of the situation, services can also be a part of a goods production process or a conventional supply chain.

The notion of a service factory also applies to service events in which the client picks up a tangible object, or receives an object resulting from a production process, as when an airline ticket is purchased at an airline terminal. So, for example, a drive-up window at a fast food restaurant is categorized as a service factory, since the client is physically located at the service facility however short the time span of the service event. In this case, however, the pick-up service is associated with a production process that results in the associated tangible object. The client obtains an object that is closely associated with the pick-up service, in contrast with the case, as covered in the next section, where the client brings in some artifact to a service shop for service and later picks it up.

A related consideration is whether the service is classified as being discrete or continuous. Hospital service is continuous consisting of a series of service events that take place over a period of time. Moreover, the service events may be dynamic in the sense that they are not necessarily planned beforehand. A doctor's visit, on the other hand, ordinarily consists of a service chain of planned events, wherein the services might include check in, get weighed, interact with the physician, and so forth, but takes place in a relatively short period of time.

Some continuous services, such as insurance and banking, incorporate a service factory that is closely associated with the provider but not the client. Clearly, services of this type have a service initiation, service agreements, and eventually a termination; but in-between service events are dynamic in the sense that they may occur on an unscheduled and unplanned basis.

Still other services in this category may utilize more than one service facility, such as a check-in terminal and a transportation vehicle. However, the classification applies since the client occupies provider facilities for the duration of the service, even though those facilities may be physically distinct. Banking with multiple service branches is a form of continuous service with more than one service facility.

## *The Service Shop*

In a second instance, some services involve leaving a possession of the client at a service shop for later pick-up, as in the cases of dry cleaning and auto repair. Clearly, the service shop is associated with the service provider, and it is the service object, owned by the client, that occupies physical space in the service facility for the duration of the service process.

### The Service Portal

Some services engage a virtual service facility for the duration of the service event. All of this sounds like the Internet, and that's the idea. (Actually, the Internet is the communications facility, and the World Wide Web (WWW) software is the service provider.) However, the category also includes telecommuting and a variety of online and telephone services. In fact, any activity, generally classed as e-Commerce, falls under the umbrella of a service portal. Included in the category of service portals is a variety of information services and "do it yourself" activities. An interesting phenomenon exists concerning the metaphorical conception of the World Wide Web (WWW). Maglio and Matlock (Maglio, 1998) interviewed beginning and experienced web users and determined that people naturally think of the web as a physical space in which they move to get things done. So, even though the web is not physical, users – that is, clients in the service domain – conceptually travel to the service provider.

### Mobile Service Facilities

In the previous categories, the emphasis has been on provider resources that occupy a fixed space, incorporating personnel, buildings, equipment, machines, vehicles, and supplies. The scenario has been that the client travels to the service facility or accesses it via some modern convenience. There are also services wherein the provider travels to a third party location to perform a service for a client, such as car washing. In this form of service, the provider travels to a location, such as a parking lot, where the service is performed, and the facilities necessary to do the job are brought along with the provider. Various forms of road service additionally fall into this category.

In other cases, the client moves as in navigation services and various forms of satellite communication, such as radio, information providing, and related services – such as car unlocking – travel with the client.

### Client Facilities

The subject of service provisioning would not be complete without the mention of client facilities, as in the case where the service provider travels to the client to perform a service, such as personal training, lawn care, cleaning, landscaping, and so forth. In most instances in this group, the service is performed on a possession of the client and not on the client itself.

## Service Implementation

All organizations and all persons do not have the same service requirements and accordingly, the same problems. Moreover, it is impossible to look at services from solely an industry perspective or even a personal point of view. Clearly, services differ between industries and between persons. On the other hand, the diverse set of activities universally called *services* wouldn't be called *services* if there weren't some degree of commonality among them. Accordingly, we are going to take a look at steps in the service process, not necessarily service interactions, per se, that are commonly incorporated into the service chain. Next, we will take a look at operations that are specific to a particular service.

It is necessary and important to emphasize the difference between generic functions performed to sustain a service – any service – and specific operations performed to achieve a particular purpose. In the former case, we are dealing with steps that support a service process including: initiation, entry administration, service interactions, termination, exit administration, and archiving. Some of the functions are not present in all services, or they are implicit in an informal service arrangement. In many cases, the generic functions necessary for sustaining services can be viewed as organizational activities.

Service *initiation* refers to the steps necessary to schedule a service and establish a provider/client interaction. Appointments with professional service providers are normally scheduled, whereas arrangements with nonprofessionals are commonly scheduled on an informal basis. Some service providers use appointments to manage demand as a means of achieving service efficiency. Entry service *administration* initiates customer input, such as filling out forms, and establishes a service agreement encompassing fees and expectations. Legal documents may be involved with this step, and client requirements are delineated. Service *interactions* are the steps in the service process. For discrete service processes, service interactions are statically planned with expected variations, since most services are customized by the provider for each client. For continuous service processes, service interactions are dynamically engaged – as in the case of banking, insurance, and hospital care. Service *termination* represents the end of a set of service interactions, regardless of whether they are statically or dynamically executed. Follow-on services or referrals are established during this step. Exit service *administration* initiates the record-keeping process and deals with the economic aspects of the service process. Service *archiving* handles information storage and legal requirements.

Collectively, the six generic functions are normally present, explicitly or implicitly, in practically all service processes, and are referred to as the *service platform*. The intended meaning of the terminology is that the service platform supports the service process.

# Business Service Systems

The basis of business service systems is the evolution from collaboration to automation. The first phase, entitled *Collaboration*, utilizes human engineering principles and is characterized as "assistance by doing some of the work." The next phase, entitled *Augmentation*, utilizes technology to increase productivity by using tools to supplement human activity. The third phase, entitled *Delegation*, is the outsourcing to service providers of non-core business processes that do not provide competitive advantage for the service provider. The final phase, entitled *Automation*, employs technology to provide self-service systems. Employing the four elements of business service systems, namely organization, technology, management, and information systems, service businesses can move among the phases by considering the following elements: business value (*Should we?*), technology (*Can we?*), governance (*May we?*), and business priorities (*Will we?*).

## *Globalization*

A business service system is a complex socio-techno-economic system that combines people, technology, value, and clients along four dimensions: information sharing, work sharing, risk sharing, and goods sharing. (Maglio, 2007, and Maglio and Spohrer, 2007) There is some evidence that some elements of all four dimensions are present in all business service systems. Before globalization, services were performed between provider and client with a high degree of locality. After Globalization Three (Friedman, 2006), business value is created through services that are shared across organizational and international boundaries. Information and communications technology (ICT) is the key business driver in value creation and is the form of technology most closely aligned with business service systems.

## *Information and Communications Technology*

ICT is the latest in a long chain of buzzwords intended to refer to what business, government, and education do with computers. The most interesting implication of the acronym ICT, however, is that the availability of computers and communications to do just about any digital job we can think of is taken for granted. In a real sense, it is the application of technology to the co-creation of value by the interaction of provider and client, without requiring that the service participants be in the same location. On-line shopping is a noteworthy example of a service that creates value for both the seller and the buyer.

An information system is a collection of hardware, software, databases, telecommunications facilities, people, and operational procedures designed to collect, manipulate, store, process, and communicate data among components of an enterprise. An information system, sometimes known as a computer-based information system, is a service provider and its clients are the people, employees, business partners, and even other information systems in that application domain. As a multidimensional service provider, an information system is a platform for the nationalization and globalization of services. The effect of ICT is not restricted to information alone. Through ICT, multinational supply chains, to give only one example, are not only possible, but desirable.

The effectiveness of ICT is, of course, directly related to the Internet, because it lowers the cost of operating on a national and international scale. Consumers and enterprises alike can operate in a global marketplace to obtain lower costs for goods and services on a 24/7 schedule. Clearly, low-cost suppliers and service providers are available globally. The use of ICT in service provisioning is more closely associated with business services than it is with personal and domestic services. Large organizations experience an enormous reduction in communications costs through the effective use of ICT.

Use of the Internet as a communications platform is not without its drawbacks. The ubiquitous nature of Internet service lends itself to problems with cybersecurity, since most facilities have a global availability.

## Collaborative Services

Just about everything we do in the modern world involves having someone else do part of the process for us. In most cases, specialization runs the show, and another person or organization can do a better job and at a lower price. This is a tricky subject, since all forms of collaboration do not benefit both parties. When one organization has a facility – such as cheap labor or certain materials – that another party does not have, then both organizations benefit. The assembly of specialized parts of an automobile engine is a prime example. But if a franchised organization, such as fast food, is required to purchase supplies by contract from the home office, then both parties do not necessarily benefit.

### *Outsourcing*

*Outsourcing* is the transfer of the ownership of a business process to a supplier, which includes management and day-to-day execution of that function. The most common functions that are outsourced are information technology, human resources, accounting, customer support, and call center operations. The key characteristics of outsourcing are "transfer" and ownership; it is different from the process in which the buyer retains control and tells the supplier how to do the work. The objective of outsourcing can be and often is one of the following: reducing costs, focusing the capability of a particular business on more profitable activities, and to obtain special capabilities that the provider firm may possess. Core business competencies are usually not outsourced. For example, airlines commonly outsource telephone reservation and information systems to foreign companies in order to reduce costs and focus on flight operations. Another example, more close to home, is the outsourcing of business cleaning services to benefit from economies of scale for that type of service.

With outsourcing, the client and the provider enter into a business relationship, established with a substantial business agreement, and then the service provider takes over the business process. Outsourcing is frequently associated with offshoring, covered next, but that is not a definitive characteristic.

### Offshoring

*Offshoring* is a general term that describes the relocation of a business process from one country to another. Although the present context is services, the practice also applies to manufacturing and production, because they are essentially services. If a country can provide services in a less expensive manner than other countries, it gives them a comparative advantage to freely trade those services.

To be more specific, offshoring is the practice of transferring an internal business process of a company in one country to another country, to be executed by the same or a different company. Service offshoring is particularly appealing to modern business since many services involve ICT, thereby facilitating inter-country relocation.

Offshoring may involve the transfer of intellectual property and training to the receiving country and is related to the availability of educated and trained labor as factors in production – the others being land and capital. According, many design and development services have been redirected offshore.

### Outsourcing and Offshoring

It follows from the above discussion that a company that engages in the transfer of an entire business function to another company in another country is both outsourcing and offshoring. As mentioned previously, common examples of outsourcing are call centers, accounting, customer support, human relations, and information technology (IT). It is now appropriate to add medical diagnosis, design services, and engineering services to the list and recognize that both outsourcing and offshoring are involved.

Public opinion on combined outsourcing and offshoring (O&O) is negative, because it is generally felt that the process adversely affects individuals and the total labor market. Even in cases in which O&O is associated with lower jobless rates, it is felt that O&O tends to shift displaced workers into lower paying jobs.

### Transformational Outsourcing

Many executives feel that outsourcing allows the firm to concentrate on core competencies and, such as the case of ICT, achieve greater flexibility. Because many business processes are totally dependent upon computers, business agility is necessary for developing responsiveness in the marketplace. *Transformational outsourcing* refers to the combination of cost saving with the potential for strategic flexibility and supplements cost focus with opportunity focus.

The underlying idea is that through transformational outsourcing, the firm will be transformed into one with the requisite characteristics for a given operational environment. Innovation in supplying services is required, therefore, because services are almost always customized and are labor intensive. Moreover, competition in the services marketplace does not tend to drive down process and profit margins.

The key point, of course, is that outsourced services do not usually provide differentiation in the marketplace. When a person purchases an automobile, for example, the buyer normally doesn't care a whole lot about where a particular component is produced.

### *Mass Production*

Many forms of service are mass produced. The assembly of military aircraft, for example, operates under a strict time schedule and penalties are assessed if schedules are not strictly met. If a supplier, for some reason or another, cannot supply a part or component on schedule, then the prime contractor has to make the item by itself. Otherwise, delays would exist all the way up the line.

### *Sharing*

The major tenet of services is that the provider and the client co-produce a service event and the composite interaction creates value for both of the participants. Four forms of sharing have been identified: information sharing, work sharing, risk sharing, and goods sharing. To a greater or lesser degree, a service is enacted by sharing. *Information sharing* is more closely aligned with services in which persons interact, such as medical provisioning and consulting. *Work sharing* is characterized by outsourcing. *Risk sharing* (although not covered so far) is associated with a continuous form of service, such as insurance, and is related to transformational outsourcing. *Goods sharing* is usually involved with certain tangible people-oriented services, such as hotels and auto rental.

### *Composite Services*

It is conceivable that a firm will want to transfer certain in-house operations to another country to reduce costs and take advantage of specific labor conditions. This process, sometimes known as FDI, or Foreign Direct Investment, allows the firm to maintain control while achieving the aforementioned benefits. From that point, it is a short step from inside offshoring to outside offshoring.

Another outsourcing possibility is to transfer equipment and personnel to the supplier, along with the business process, as in the case of some companies that have transferred their total ICT operations to an outside company. Many people feel, however, that the transferred personnel have a lower level of job security in their new employment environment.

Finally, chapter one covered the case where services exist at two or more levels, as in the airline example. In this example, the outsourced and off-shored service company enter into a service agreement with the airline to deliver information and reservation services to passengers. In this instance, the service provider has two clients: the airline and the passengers, with no stake in the eventual outcome except as governed in the service level agreement. Service packages in this category have serious drawbacks in the area of service quality and customer retention.

## Service Process Organization

Practically everyone has heard of or experienced service providers that traditionally have clients backed up with very long waiting times. A common example is the "not so fast" fast-food restaurant. In the world of services, organization is everything.

While it is literally impossible to solve all service problems in a few pages, it is feasible to deliver an organizational design that is relevant to most service systems. A definition of a service system is:

> A *service system* is a system of people and technology that adapts to the changing value of information in the system.

It is important to emphasize that the "changing value of information" also refers to the service process itself. So it should be expected that a particular service organization would adjust to changing conditions in the workplace.

In the production of goods, a measure of organization is the level of inventory, even though the management of inventory can be a subject in its own right. With services, capacity is a key element, and long waiting lines are evidence of insufficient service capacity, ineffective demand management, or inadequate organization.

In this section, a working model of service organization is presented that should serve as a starting point for looking at organizational issues.

### *An Organization Example – Retailing and Services*

The importance of service organization is inherent in retailing. Retailing is a service, as covered previously, and the sales service event changes the ownership attribute of a product. A significant aspect of retailing exists, however, that is associated with the organization of service.

There is a component in retailing that is directly related to the level of expected service as a function of the price of the product. Most customers possess a nominal price for a given product. If the sales price is lower than nominal value, then less service is expected. If the sales price is higher than the nominal price, then more service is expected or the product is deemed to be overpriced. Buyer behavior, therefore, is governed by a combination of price and retail service, so that buyer behavior is influenced to some degree by service organization.

### *Service, Service Providers, and Service Process*

Clearly, there is a difference between a service and its service provider. In doctoring, the service is the medical attention afforded the patient, and the service provider is the doctor. In auto maintenance and repair, the service provider is the dealership and the service process is the well-known service event, involving the service advisor, service technician, and a whole host of other providers.

Accordingly, the *service process* is the following set of steps in the service chain, mentioned previously: service initiation, entry administration, service interactions, service termination, and service archiving. This is a generic set of steps, and each particular form of service has its own set of provisional operations. We will develop a service organization model based on the given generic service chain.

It is important to recognize that in covering the subject of service process organization, we are going up a level in service provisioning. Most forms of service go through a sequence of steps – a form of transitional services – where some of the steps are established by the service provider and are not part of the service event, per se.

The service organization model introduced here is called the "transitional service organization" and an auto service arrangement is used as an example.

### *Transitional Service Organization Model*

In a transitional form of service organization, the service process from the client's and service provider's viewpoints consists of the following steps. (1) The owner (client) makes an appointment for service with the appointment scheduler (the demand manager). (2) The client brings the car (service object) to the dealership for service. (3) The client interacts with the service advisor (service facilitator) to exchange service particulars. (4) The client waits for service or leaves the dealership's premises (the service factory). (5) The service arrangement is entered into a computer (the service scheduler) by the service facilitator. (6) The service technician (the server) subsequently picks up the service order and performs the required service, often coordinating with the service facilitator for additional information. (7) The server registers the service completion with the service scheduler. (8) The service scheduler sends a request to the service administrator for billing. (9) The client interacts with the service administrator for pickup and payment resolution, and the service event is completed.

The service model consists of five key relationships: governance, information, service, ownership, and the service-level agreement. Additionally, there are nine major components: the service provider, the service client, the service manager, the service facilitator, the service scheduler, the service server, the service object, the demand manager, and the service administrator. Each element is considered in detail in a subsequent chapter on the business of services.

The model applies to the three major forms of service: people processing, possession processing, and information services.

## Quick Summary

1. A service system is a system of people and technology that adapts to the changing value of knowledge in the system. The participants in a service system are the provider and client and the relationship between them is the service process. Systems of this type require an environment in which to operate that can take the form of a service factory in which the client resides for the duration of the service process and the service shop in which a possession of the client resides for the duration of the service event.

2. Service systems are facilitated by information and communications technology and enhanced by globalization. Service provisioning is inherent in outsourcing and offshoring. Innovation in supplying services is required because services are usually customized and labor intensive.

3. Core business processes are not customarily outsourced, and outsourcing predominantly does not provide differentiation in the marketplace.

4. The transitional service organization model demonstrates the commonality and variability of service systems, and gives rise to three proposed laws of service systems: people processing, possession processing, and information services.

## Key Terms

The reader should be familiar with the following terms in the context in which they were used in the chapter.

| | |
|---|---|
| Augmentation | Service object |
| Client facilities | Service platform |
| Collaboration | Service portal |
| Delegation | Service process |
| ICT | Service shop |
| Mobile service facility | Service system |
| Offshoring | Transformational outsourcing |
| Outsourcing | Transitional services |
| Service factory | |

## Selected Reading

Friedman, T. (2006). *The World is Flat: A Brief History of the Twenty-First Century*, New York: Farrar, Straus and Giraux.

Sowa, J. (2000). *Knowledge Representation: Logical, Philosophical and Computational Foundations*, Brooks Cole Publishing, Pacific Grove Publishing, Inc.

*Offshoring* (2007). http://en.wikipedia.org/wiki/Offshoring.

*Ontology* (2007). http://en.wikipedia.org/wiki/Ontology.

*Outsourcing* (2007). http://en.wikipedia.org/wiki/Outsourcing.

Maglio, P. (2007). *Service Science, Management, and* Engineering (SSME)*: An Interdisciplinary Approach to Service Innovation*, IBM Almaden Research Center, http://almaden.ibm.com/ssme, p. 14.

IBM Almaden Services Research. (2006). *Service Science, Management, and* Engineering (SSME)*: Challenges, Frameworks, and Call for Participation*, http://almaden.ibm.com/ssme, p. 13.

Maglio, P. and Spohrer, J. (2007). *Fundamentals of Service Science*, IBM Almaden Research Center.

Maglio, P. and Matlock, T. (1998). *Metaphors We Surf the Web By*, The Information Architecture Institute.

# 3

## INFORMATION SERVICE

Through information and communications technology, modern society has made enormous advances in how we live and work. How far we have progressed is summarized by Microsoft chairman Bill Gates in a recent email message: "The ability to access and share information instantly and communicate in ways that transcend the boundaries of time and distance has given rise to an era of unprecedented productivity and innovation that has created new economic opportunities for hundreds of millions of people around the world and paved the way for global growth that is unparalleled in human history."

### Information Service Concepts

An *information service* is a resource capable of supporting a service event or instantiating a service event based on information. In other words, an information service can assist in the execution of a service, such as in retailing, or it can actually be the service as when buying a pair of shoes over the Internet – actually, it is the World Wide Web, but that distinction is not required at this point. The resource is a service provider that can take the form of a person or a computer. The execution of an information service event requires a service client that can take the form of a person or computer, and the provider and client must interact in order to co-produce the service. The execution of a service event changes the state of the provider and the client, but a tangible object is not produced. An information service is commonly associated with computer technology, but that is not a necessary condition. The most definitive characteristic of an information service is that the information travels, which gives rise to new models of information management and communications technology.

### *A Personal Dimension*

Most of the information that is communicated between people is about something. When you buy a car, the sales person tells you about the key features and how to use them. In the physician/patient relationship, the doctor and patient exchange information about a medical situation. Clearly, there is some form of informational interchange that accompanies practically all services. Information service is more than the incidental exchange of information.

With information services, the client specifically requests information and the provider supplies it using some form of communications channel. The service request may be implicit in some other form of activity or it may be "ordered" on a demand basis, but it is nevertheless requested.

### *Data versus Information*

Each provider/client interaction in an information service requires a context, and here is why. Pure unadulterated facts are known as *data*. For example, the date April 15th can mean different things to different people. To many Americans, it means tax day. To others, it may be the start of the baseball season. To grandmother, it may be her birth date. *Information* is data in a particular context so it has a specific meaning.

When you request some information about a subject from an Internet web site, for example, the context is supplied in some manner, such as from the site itself, the nature of the query, or even information in a previously requested web page. The context effectively gives meaning to data and turns it into information. The bits that flow through wires or through the air as electromagnetic radiation are nothing more than data, at best. Accordingly, it would be proper to say that it is an information service that turns a bunch of bits into something useful, such as a news story or downloaded music.

### Ordinary Mail

Not all information services necessarily require a computer. The United States Postal Service is a case in point, as is its international equivalent, known as the PTT (Post, Telephone, and Telegraph), which do not require a computer in their basic form. Electronic mail (email as we generally know it) is also an information service, and it does require a computer. Each element has a sender and an intended recipient.

Who is the service provider? It is certainly not the sender or recipient. Clearly, it is the mail service itself. If you're thinking that the mail service is the communications channel, then you are on the right track. In this instance, and this instance only, the sender and receiver are the clients and the mail service is the service provider. In most other information services, the communications channel *is* only the channel for communication and nothing more. With mail service, pickup, transportation, and delivery would appear to be the service, and the informational content of the message is not brought into the analysis.

*Harry Katzan Jr.*

### Is Software a Service?

Yes. Software would appear to be a service, such as in document preparation and as suggested by a case of ordinary mail. Information is moved from one place to another, and perhaps it is transformed a bit in the process. In document preparation, or word processing, as it is usually called, information is moved from an origin, such as a person's brain, through the nervous system, the person's fingers, and the keyboard to the computer and software and then to a document file. Nevertheless, it is transferred from one place to another. If electronic mail is considered to be a service, then it would seem that word processing is also. Consider another example. If you go to a tax preparation agency to have your return prepared, you consider it to be a service. If you buy a program for a small fee that does the same work as the tax agency, does it perform a service? Most people would agree that tax software is a service. In the same vein, presentation, spreadsheet, and database software would also be regarded as services.

There is another aspect to all of this, as exemplified by the word processing and email examples. The provider and client participate in the exchange of information, even though they may not be, and probably won't be, in close proximity. Thus, the distance metric is not necessarily significant in word processing, and in the case of email, even the time metric is also not significant.

Is *all* software a service? Perhaps, that should have been the original question. It is an open item. It is easy to conceptualize that office software for document preparation, presentation, graphics, data management, and data analysis could be regarded as services, since that software facilitates the transfer of information from one place to another and also modifies its precise format. In the area of information systems, DSS (Decision Support System) software, for example, provides timely information to managers to aid in decision making. DSS software is definitely a service. What about AI (Artificial Intelligence) software, such as software that monitors gauges in a nuclear reactor? Then, if something goes wrong, the computer program shuts the reactor down before a meltdown occurs. Again, most people, especially those that work in nuclear power plants, would agree that it is a service. The debate could go on. For this chapter, at least, software is a service.

Practically speaking, a software package, by itself, does not qualify to be an information service. In order to function as a service, software must be operating on a computer in order to respond to a client's request in an appropriate manner. You always need a computer and communications infrastructure to support software services.

## Enterprise Information Services

Information is the cornerstone of modern business, and government as well, and is the major ingredient in everyday commerce. In the study of information services, the distinction between information and the system to handle the information is often blurred. In this section, we will establish the difference between information and services.

A lot of information is about things: about a product or service, about travel arrangements, about how to do something, about an event, about a person or group, about something that has happened in the past, and so forth. We are going to refer to this type of information as *operand information*, and we are additionally going to refer to information that is involved with the service process itself as *operant information*. (Vargo and Lusch, 2007) When the focus of an information service is the result, then as Vargo and Lusch might put it, we are using goods-dominant logic and the result is referred to as the operand. When the focus of an information service is on the process, then we are employing service-dominant logic and the operant resources are the information and the other steps in the service process.

## Business Information

Business information services are usually divided into two categories: operational services and management services. Operational services are employed to run the enterprise and management services are used to manage the enterprise. Some of the same basic concepts are used in both categories, but the time and distance characteristics are different. For example, a database management system and a database are normally used to store persistent data for the enterprise. With operational services, the database is dynamic and is updated for each transaction. With management services, static data is needed to make effective decisions. Accordingly, a static database would ordinarily be created from the dynamic database so that timely management reports could be generated. Of course, this is a bit of a simplification, but the basic idea is there.

The management of information is an enterprise service in its own right. Clearly, the transfer of information from operational databases to a data warehouse is a concrete example of an enterprise information service.

## Transaction Services

When you make an airline reservation or check a flight schedule using the Internet, you are using a transaction processing system. Most information services that support operational systems in today's world use transaction processing, comprised of the following elements: client computer, communication channel, server computer, communications channel, flight operations computer, and flight database.

At the most general level, you interact with the server using the communications channel. You are the client, the server is the provider, and the service is the transaction. The communications channel between the passenger's computer and the server is probably the Internet. The second communications channel could be the Internet or a dedicated network. Some people call this channel the *service bus*; we will go into more detail on this subject shortly. The server computer is a client to the flight reservations computer, which is the service provider and whatever request the former makes to the latter is the service. In a similar vein, the database management system provides a service to the flight reservation computer. The entire process is mediated by hardware and software and the only thing that moves is the information.

## *Information Processing*

Fundamental to all the modern-day hype about the Internet, social networking, and online collaboration is the much maligned subject of data processing, or as it is now called in the modern world "information processing." *Information processing* is what computers do to sustain business operations and comprise what we will refer to as the operant of the information service process. Information systems are the hardware, software, communications, organizational, and human facilities that sustain information processing. There are macro operations (as in macro economics) such as accessing records, sorting records, merging records, storing records, manipulating records, and reporting; and there are micro operations (again as in micro economics) such as reading, writing, moving, and performing arithmetic operations on specific pieces of data. Collectively, macro and micro operations are the substance of information services.

An effective information service requires effective information that is usually taken to mean that the information is timely, accurate, complete, relevant, accessible, verifiable, and reliable. The attributes of information determine the efficacy of an information service.

### *Client and Provider Input to an Information Service*

An information service requires client and provider input, just as in any other kind of service. Usually, the client – whether it is a person or a computer – enters a small amount of information into the service process. The provider – usually a computer information system – has access to a larger store of information, so that we can say the provider provisionally supplies a larger amount of information. The informational output of an information service is a function of the inputs and the nature of the service.

The client may have help supplying input to an information service through hardware and software facilities known as "interaction services." The provider may have assistance from database services and auxiliary services via a service bus.

### *Interaction Services*

Most people are familiar with user-friendly graphical user interfaces, known as GUIs. Desktop environments and web pages are common examples. An *interaction service* is a familiar idiom for interacting with a computer. Clearly, this is a client's point of view. An interaction service is normally a socially-constructed collection of structural elements and behavioral patterns, such as action buttons, list boxes, and pull-down menus. The idea is to get information into the computer in the most efficient manner, and there are two basic methods: a command-line interface and a GUI interface. The command-line interface demands textual input and is great for a wide range of technical environments. For most clients, a GUI interface is superior, but each form of GUI requires a well-defined group of clients.

The software and hardware combination that supports client input is known as a "thin client" or a "thick client." With a *thin client*, the software for information service interaction is minimal and is usually limited to facilities provided with the computer platform that the client is using. With a *thick client*, the software for user interaction is more extensive and is tuned to a particular group of information services.

Interaction services are dependent upon what the client expects to do with the information service. Here are some examples:

- Information exploration (e.g., find out about service)
- Accomplish something (e.g., reserve a seat)
- Find a "good enough" answer to a question (e.g., how do we get to New York)
- Change the direction of a search operation (e.g., what about service systems)
- Establish a point of reference (e.g., mark my place to come back to at a later time)

Designing effective interaction services is not so easy but one approach is to think about the elements with which you have to work. A common set of such elements is composed of objects (such as icons), actions (such as a file menu), subject (such as the information that you have to work with), and tools (such as calendars and appointments).

Interaction services are a small part of service, but nevertheless an important part.

### Service Bus

A *service bus* is a high-speed data link between two computing platforms that operate in a request/response mode. The client requests an item of information (such as the price of IBM stock on Monday at 11:00 on a given date) and the provider, which operates in a server mode, supplies it in an expeditious manner. A service bus requires software that is called *middleware*.

An example of the need for a service bus is inherent in the following example. A stock broker is on a line to a client who requests the price of IBM stock. The brokerage firm has a computer (the server) that gets an up-to-the-second feed from the stock exchange. There is a high speed link between the stock brokers and the server, and each broker has a specialized thick client interface. The broker enters the stock symbol for IBM into a text box and clicks a send button. The server responds in a fraction of a second with the requested price.

### Collaboration

Teams are the accepted norm in the modern service enterprise, and collaboration is the process by which they progress toward a common goal. With information services, collaboration between groups and individuals can be managed from geographically dispersed locations. In general, collaboration has a well-defined structure and set of operational procedures that employs any or all of four recursive information service modalities: email, instant messaging, interactive media, and specially designed collaborative software.

Collaboration operates at the intellectual level and often benefits from decentralization and varying degrees of academic and personal diversity. Collaboration is a unique form of service. The service provider in the information service modality is established through information and communications technology, and is an instance of where the "service is the service provider," because it allows the clients in a collaboration service to exchange meaningful information.

Collaboration requires at least two clients interacting in what is referred to as a *multiclient service*. A multiclient service is frequently leaderless and is known as a *virtual organization structure*. Traditional workflow where a document is passed between team members is a common form of collaboration.

## Information Service Applications

The range of information services is multidimensional and ubiquitous, and touches on virtually all aspects of everyday life. It would seem that everything affects everything, and the medium of exchange is information. Looking at the big picture, the three big players are people, business, and government. People interact with themselves and with business and government to engage in commerce, obtain information and services, and to participate in various forms of interpersonal communication. Businesses interact with people, other businesses, and the government to make a profit. The government interacts with other governmental entities, as well as people and businesses to provide a requisite level of service. The fuel that feeds the fire is information, which is sustained by the environment, technology, economics, and society. In the world of the Internet and the World Wide Web, information services are paramount.

### *Pull versus Push*

It is perhaps a bit of an oversimplification, but "the manner in which you approach an information service determines what you get." The characteristics of the *pull model* are succinctly summarized in the following sentence. "Rather than 'push,' this new approach focuses on 'pull' – creating platforms that help people to mobilize appropriate resources when the need arises."

Push models are essentially scripted and thrive in stable environments with little uncertainty. Forecasting, as in demand forecasting, is key in push environments and allows high levels of efficiency to be developed in business processes. Most of modern business and governmental activity uses the push modality. A business pushes a product into the marketplace and people buy it.

Push programs are top-down processes with the following steps: design, deploy, execute, monitor, and refine.

Pull models increase value creation for both clients and providers. For clients, "pull" activity expands the scope of available resources. For providers, pull systems expand the market for services. Pull platforms are associated with the following attributes: uncertain demand, emergent design, decentralized environment, loosely coupled modular construction of facilities, and on-demand service provisioning. Pull models are more amenable to uncertain business conditions.

From both the client's and the provider's perspectives, pull services focus on the following activities: find, select, purchase, deliver, and service. If all of this sounds familiar, it should be. It represents how you buy shoes on the Internet.

### *Enterprise Service Constituents*

The seven constituents of an enterprise information service are providers, clients, messages, communications, information processing, persistent storage, and the user interface that collectively take into consideration the requisite technology including database facilities, email archives, protocols, business rules, operational procedures, and a variety of service interactions needed for enterprise applications. Since information and not people move in information services, this category of service is based on information and communications technology. It is important that when we discuss information services at the enterprise level, we are primarily concerned with functionality and not necessarily with computing platforms.

### *Information Service Model*

Information service systems typically operate in a client/server mode, which means that the end user is the service client, the enterprise application running on a computing platform is the service provider, and the means of client and provider interaction is some form of communications channel. Typically, the client enters information into the system through a well-defined interface and the provider does something in return. Exactly what the provider does is of primary importance to the information service system.

There are at least three distinct possibilities:

1. The provider accesses some form of persistent storage and returns selected information to the client.
2. The provider performs some element of information processing and returns an indicator to the client that it was done.
3. The client and the provider enter into an interactive dialog concerning specific informational elements and a supply chain operation is initiated to accomplish the corresponding enterprise operation.

As such, information service systems are instrumental in supporting daily activities. Typical business applications are order processing, purchasing, accounting, inventory control, human resources, marketing and sales support, manufacturing, and various forms of service support including data collection and information management.

An *enterprise resource planning* (ERP) service is an integrated collection of constituent applications operating at the enterprise level that provide information services in six comprehensive areas: production, supply chain, customer relationship management, sales support and ordering, financial and managerial accounting, and human resources. An ERP service essentially operates by using a cross section of diverse traditional business applications to satisfy client requests for information and is particularly appropriate to a global environment.

## Scope of Electronic Information Services

It is possible to be more definitive about electronic information services. Three entities are involved: Business (B), Government (G), and the consumer (C). The interactions are delineated as follows: B2C means business-to-consumer, B2B means business-to-business, G2B means government-to-business, C2C means consumer-to-consumer, G2G means government-to-government, and G2C means government-to-consumer. In the symbols, the leftmost letter reflects the provider and the rightmost letter represents the client.

### *Electronic Commerce*

Electronic commerce is an enterprise information service application supported by the Internet and the World Wide Web, and can be viewed as an opportunistic means of doing business with minimal cost. In short, the information services of the Internet and the Web are used to conduct business.

Electronic commerce is usually known as e-commerce or B2C for short. Conventional business establishments are referred to as "brick and mortar" facilities characterized by a shopping area in which customers can view products, and business personnel can conduct commerce. The equivalent in the digital world is an e-commerce web site where a consumer can conduct analogous functions, usually via a GUI interface. The service provider is the e-commerce web site and the customer is the client connected to the web site via the Internet. In this instance, the Internet is the communications channel. The service process is the set of interactions between the customer and one or more web sites that go through the following steps: find, select, purchase, deliver, and service.

*Find* is an Internet service process, which is usually a set of service interactions, to navigate to the desired Internet retailer. After the electronic retailer is chosen, the *select* and *purchase* services represent the online equivalent of the traditional process of making a purchase. Purchasing involves payment that invokes a secure service designed for that specific purpose. *Deliver* is another service process initiated by the retailer for physically delivering the product to the consumer. *Service* is the Web-enabled service process of providing customer support. Each of the steps in the B2C service process (i.e., find, select, purchase, deliver, and service) involves at least one service, so the entire process can be properly regarded as a *multiservice*, driven by a series of constituent information services.

B2C transactions are characterized by increased convenience, enhanced efficiency, additional buying choice, and lower prices, from the consumer's perspective, and by an increased return on retailing investment for the electronic retailer. An electronic retailer need not have a related "brick and mortar" facility, but that is often the case thereby allowing that enterprise to operate in both domains.

### Electronic Business

Electronic business is the use of the Internet and the World Wide Web to conduct business operations, including intra-business and inter-business transactions. This is a broad category and ranges from relatively simple information services to obtain tacit business information from within a single organization to complex Web Services between distinct organizations.

Electronic business is usually known as e-business or B2B for short and has its roots in electronic data interchange (EDI) commonly used to exchange information on business operations within an organization, and between business partners, suppliers, and wholesalers. The use of the Internet for communications services reduces operational costs for computer networks and increases the value obtained from costs that are incurred.

The major advantage of B2B operations is that companies can utilize an information service known as the "B2B Electronic Marketplace," wherein they can buy and sell products and exchange information through a *virtual marketplace*. Not only can companies create supply chains, but they can create business partnerships in which one company can take advantage of the information services of another company. The process, known as the *componentization of information services*, facilitates the creation of web services that allow the company to be a more responsive (to market and economic conditions) enterprise.

B2B is similar to B2C in one respect. Modern company operations require the purchase of certain *indirect materials*, typically referred to as MRO materials, where MRO stands for "maintenance, repair, and operations," and include such items as ball pens, repair parts, and office equipment. Through the B2B electronic marketplace, various companies can collectively achieve lower cost through *demand aggregation* of *direct materials* that are items used in production or retail operations as part of a company's core business.

### Electronic Marketplace

Information services, such as the electronic marketplace, permit companies to engage in B2B market operations in horizontal and vertical electronic marketplaces. In a *horizontal marketplace*, buyers and sellers can interact across many industries. Travel and financial services are common examples, because they are applicable to almost any type of business, such as the process industries (oil and gas) and conventional and electronic retailing.

In a *vertical marketplace*, buyers and sellers are in the same industry and primarily engage in information services that relate to direct material utilization.

## *Electronic Government*

Information services are a means of transforming the management and operations of government to be more responsive, efficient, and reliable in delivering services to the electorate – at all governmental levels, including federal, state, and local communities. The objective is to enhance informational facilities that already exist so they may properly be regarded as click and mortar, with the options of obtaining information and services via the Internet and World Wide Web while continuing to have a physical presence. Three flavors have been identified: Government to Business (G2B), Government to Consumer (G2C), and Government to Government (G2G). In the latter case, there are two possibilities: inter-government and intra-government. Inter-government refers to the vertical alignment of information services between governmental levels on the same initiative, such as the coordination of federal, state, and local agencies on air pollution. Intra-government refers to the horizontal alignment of services between agencies at the same level of government, such as disaster response coordination between police, fire, and emergency medical departments.

Government to business operations reflect information services that cover purchasing of MRO materials, and the provisioning of information facilities for procedures, regulations, reporting, and compliance. In the latter case, governmental reporting facilities (by business to government) are commonly available to submit requisite documentation through Internet and World Wide Web services.

Most citizens are familiar with Government to consumer information services for taxes and various forms of registration. For taxpayers, the ability to download forms and directions, and the ability to submit completed tax forms is paramount. For those of us fortunate enough to receive a tax refund, the increased efficiency is money in the bank. Vehicle and voter registration are other information services that are efficient from both client and provider perspectives.

Overall, however, the availability of information on dates, procedures, directions, and so forth, at the click of a mouse via the Internet and the World Wide Web – pure information services – is the greatest advantage of G2C services.

## Personal Information Services

Personal Information services are an ever expanding collection of Internet and World Wide Web applications. The prevalence of the applications, however, brings up a fundamental question about exactly what constitutes the clients, providers, and the services in the various forms of information service. The resources appear to be different among the applications, so the presentation of the subject matter will be instructive for determining the scope of personal information services. Accordingly, we will cover the following services: chat rooms, instant messaging, Internet telephone, web auctions, user-generated media, social networking, and newsgroups. This is only a sample of relevant applications but is indicative of how information services are used to support those applications.

### *Chat Rooms*

One of the most popular means of communicating on the Internet is through a chat room, the best known of which is IRC (Internet Relay Chat). IRC operates in the client/server mode and requires an IRC server; clients require special IRC software, usually downloaded from the Internet.

When using chat, the user selects a channel, which establishes the conversation in which the user will participate. Characteristically, other users, throughout the world, will have chosen the same channel. The idea being that they will exchange information on a certain subject.

During operation, clients type messages on their local client computer and the information is relayed via the Internet to the server. The message is then forwarded to other users signed on to the same channel and is displayed on their screens. A user may just listen, figuratively speaking, or may participate in the conversation. Ostensibly, users respond to other user's transmissions, so that an identifying name (sometimes called a *handle*) accompanies each submission. Since chat rooms are a global phenomenon, a network of IRC servers is required to service all of the users in a specific domain. A recent development is "voice chat," which is an audio equivalent to the traditional text-based chat.

At the end-user level, a chat room can be viewed as a collection of clients whose interpersonal communications is being managed by the chat server system operating as a service provider. The chat server system consists of the hardware, software, and Internet facilities, necessary to do the task. The service process consists of a set of dynamically determined client/server interactions, where the end-user is the client and the chat server is the service provider.

### Instant Messaging

Instant messaging is the private real-time communication of textual messages between two users logged on to an instant messaging (IM) server over the Internet. Messages are forwarded through an IM server that uses the "sender" client's buddy list to determine the destination for forwarded messages.

Many Internet specialists consider instant messaging to be a form of chat room operations, since it has similar information service characteristics.

## *Front and Back Stages*

Internet chat and instant messaging, among other information services, incorporate a value chain of component services, divided between front and back stages. Essentially, the front stage is what the end-user conceptualizes and the back stage is what is going on under the covers, so to speak.

The noteworthy aspect of the division is that human clients are only part of the process, if they are involved at all, and the front stage represents the client's experience supplemented by the back stage that represents the information service support structure based on ICT facilities. The participants (Human or ICT) may possess different but complementary views of the service process.

## *Internet Telephone*

Using the Internet for making telephone calls is appealing to many people because of the cost, which may be free in some cases, over and above the cost of the Internet connection. Several methods and associated software facilities are available. They generally fall into two broad categories.

In the first case, you use special hardware and software to communicate through your personal computer (PC) using a microphone and speakers. If you are calling someone who is also using the same method, the call is totally free, as it is with web browsing and email, and it is also applicable to users anywhere in the world.

In the second case, you use your ordinary "land line" telephone handset, and the call is routed over the Internet using a service process generally known as Voice over IP (VoIP). With VoIP, your voice is digitized and routed through the Internet as information packets, similar to other information services such as web pages and email. At the receiving end, the voice packets are converted to normal telephone signals.

With Internet telephone, the conceptualized front and back stages coincide. The clients are the telephone users and the service provider is the value chain of Internet activities.

### *Web Auctions*

A *web auction* is an Internet and World Wide Web service that connects buyers and sellers in a consumer-to-consumer (C2C) mode to conduct an online version of traditional auction. A well-known web site that manages the web auction process is *eBay*, but there are notably other sites that perform the same service.

In this instance, the information service is the posting and delivery of information concerning products for sale and associated bids. The clients are the buyers and sellers and the information service consists of the information processing facilities to sustain the auction. In this instance, the Internet and the World Wide Web serve only as a communication channel.

### *User Generated Media*

There are three major forms of information dissemination normally originating from individuals that use the Internet and World Wide Web services: web logs, podcasts, and various information feeds. The services are related and are covered together in this section.

A *web log* (called a *blog*) is a medium for presenting information without restrictions or review over the Internet and accessible through the World Wide Web. People who participate in the service of creating information content in this category are known as *bloggers*, and the process itself is known as *blogging*. The following three information services are normally associated with this form of activity: (1) Obtaining information on how to set up and access a blog web site; (2) Providing services that assist in actually setting up a blog web site; and (3) Using services that assist in making entries in a web log. Each blog site has an Internet uniform resource locator (URL) and a theme, subsequently used for search and discovery.

Clearly, the information services needed for accessing blogs are traditional web searches, wherein you request information and it is returned to you using pull technology. Individuals use search engines, such as Google, to locate blog sites. For example, if you were interested in people's opinions on "broccoli," you would do a search with the following search phrase:

**broccoli blog**

and *voila*, you could find out what some people think about the vegetable. There are search engines designed specifically for searching blog sites.

A *podcast* is an audio blog, serviced through the Internet that serves the same purpose as a personal radio station. Using your PC and a microphone, you can record a document and store it on an appropriate blog site. Other users can then download the audio blog to their PC for listening or for transfer to a music player. Podcasts are used to listen to broadcast media and educational material. In the latter category, a podcast is an effective means of delivering course material to students.

An *RSS feed* is a means of generating a wider audience for blogs and podcasts, through an Internet technique known as Really Simple Syndication. RSS feeds utilize special web formatted material and delivers automatically generated downloads to registered end users using push technology.

User-generated media operations are generally considered to be a front stage process. All communications are *asynchronous*, which means they are created (or uploaded) as a process at one time and accessed (or downloaded) by another process at another time, using push technology.

## *Social Networking*

Social networking is usually regarded as the process of keeping up with friends and family, and it is no surprise that the process has migrated to the World Wide Web. The inherent information service in social networking is known as "shared space."

A *shared space* is an online virtual public space in which a person – commonly a young person – can display information about themselves, including text, audio, and video. Special web sites, such as MySpace and Facebook, are designed to handle social networking. Actually, the video is predominantly photographs taken with a digital camera and uploaded to an appropriate web site set up for social networking.

A person's virtual space is subsequently accessible by friends. The conceptual model for a shared space is that of a private room to which one can invite friends to look around, thus giving the owner a private virtual space not otherwise available in everyday life.

As with information services that support media, social networking services are asynchronous and use pull technology.

## *Newsgroups*

A *newsgroup* is a collection of people that participate in a discussion on a particular subject using Internet facilities. The usual form of communication is email, and the mode of communication is question and answer. The largest and most widely known online news group is *usenet.*

A participant subscribes to a particular topic. When that participant logs on to the newsgroup server, the entries on the selected topic are automatically sent to that participant.

Special client software is required to participate in a newsgroup. User interactions are organized by thread, so that a given user effectively engages in a conversation, as required, with participants in the same interest group. If a thread is *moderated*, questions are sent to a human moderator who screens the questions for appropriateness. Otherwise, questions are simply listed by topic. Most threads are archived by date.

Newsgroup software employs the same information service modality as email, and in fact, is dependent upon email for its operational infrastructure. Newsgroup facilities are also available through most information service portals, such as America Online and Google. With Google, you can access newsgroups via http://groups.google.com.

## Quick Summary

1. An *information service* is a resource capable of supporting a service event or instantiating in a service event based on information. In other words, an information service can assist in the execution of a service, such as in retailing, or it can actually be the service as when buying a pair of shoes on the Internet

2. Most of the information that is communicated between people is about something. With information services, the client requests information, and the provider supplies it using some form of communications channel.

3. Software would appear to be a service, such as in document preparation and as suggested by the example of ordinary mail. Information is moved from one placed to another and perhaps it is transformed a bit in the process.

4. Information is the cornerstone of modern business, and government as well, and is the major ingredient in everyday commerce. Business information services are usually divided into two categories: operational services and management

services. Operational services are employed to run the enterprise and management services are used to manage the enterprise.

5.  When you make an airline reservation or check a flight schedule using the Internet, you are using a transaction processing system. Transaction processing systems are the cornerstone of modern business.

6.  Teams are the accepted norm in the modern enterprise, and collaboration is the process by which they progress toward a common goal. With information services, collaboration between groups and individuals can be effected from geographically dispersed locations.

7.  Major enterprise information service applications are electronic commerce, electronic business, and electronic government. Major personal information service applications are chat rooms, instant messaging, Internet telephone, web auctions, web logs, podcasts, RSS feeds, social networking, and newsgroups.

## Key Terms

The reader should be familiar with the following terms in the context in which they were used in the chapter.

| | |
|---|---|
| Artificial intelligence | Information service |
| Collaboration | Operand information |
| Data versus information | Ordinary mail |
| Decision support system | Purchase |
| Deliver | Push versus pull |
| Electronic commerce | Service bus |
| Enterprise information | Select |
| system | Software as a service |
| Find | Thick client |
| Interaction service | Thin client |

## Selected Reading

Gralla, P. (2004). *How the Internet Works*, Indianapolis, IN: Que Publishing.

Hagel, J. and Brown, J. (2007). *From Push to Pull: Emerging Models for Mobilizing Resources*, www.edgeperspectives.com.

Richardson, L. and Ruby, S. (2007). RESTful Web Services, Sebastopol, DA; O'Reilly Media, Inc.

Spohrer, J., Vargo, S., Caswell, N., and Maglio, P. (2007), *The Service System is the Basic Abstraction of Service Science*, IBM Research, Almaden Research Center, San Jose, CA, www.almaden.ibm.com/asr.

Stair, R.M. and Reynolds, G. (2008). *Principles of Information Systems: A Managerial Approach*, Boston: Thomson Course Technology.

Tabas, L. (2007). *Designing for Service Systems*, UCB iSchool Report 2007-008.

Tapscott, D. and Williams, A. (2006). *Wikinomics: How Mass Collaboration Changes Everything*, New York: Penguin Group, Inc.

Tidwell, J. (2006). *Designing Interfaces*, Sebastopol, CA: O'Reilly Media, Inc.

Vargo, S. and Lusch, B. (2007). *Service-Dominant Logic Basics*, www.sdlogic.net.

# 4

---

# SERVICE MANAGEMENT

Historically, the focus of service management has been on the application of traditional management concepts to enterprise processes that primarily involve services. Typical business examples are banking and health care that have greatly benefited from the application of scientific principles to everyday operations. Two common applications are the use of waiting-line methods for the front office and process scheduling techniques for the back office. Through the application of information and communications technology (ICT), many organizations have adjusted everyday operations enabling them to go through a transformational process to achieve revenue growth by being able to respond more quickly to changing market conditions and by being more effective and efficient in the application of services. This chapter describes modern services management. The viewpoint taken here is that services management employs computer concepts, but its domain is by no means restricted to computer-based services and includes just about any service that a person can imagine.

## Service Management Concepts

There are three forces operating in the sphere of service processes. The first is the use of ICT as an enabler in providing revenue growth, efficiency, and effectiveness for traditional and enhanced services, as well as for conventional business processes. This subject is commonly referred to as information systems. The second is the consulting services domain that provides IT services to external organizations. The third is the use of ICT to manage information systems and services, which is a field of endeavor known as IT Services Management. Briefly said, it is the use of ICT to manage the total enterprise including its computer services.

### *Information Technology*

Information Technology (IT), as a discipline, has been around for a while and has heretofore been regarded as computer hardware and software in support of both personal and enterprise activities. With widespread acceptance of the Internet, the World Wide Web, and advanced information systems, as well as enhanced personal productivity aids, the abbreviation has taken on a more inclusive meaning to include all of the activities mentioned, in addition to many organizational and workforce assets. When most modern executives refer to IT, as in "We will have to increase the IT budget for next year," they are referring to people, technology, and organization.

### *Domain of Service Management*

Many people feel that what you see in the world depends on the lens through which you are looking. So if you adopt a service-centric point of view, most socially-developed phenomena can be viewed as services. It follows that if we are going to manage services, we should at least consider to whom services are applied and how excellent service delivery is achieved.

We are going to focus on an organizational setting consisting of people and everyday operational units. The *service provider*, in this instance, is a person acting in a service capacity or a group of persons, including support facilities, that has adopted a role of a service provider. The *service object* is another person or operational unit, usually referred to as a *business unit*. In the latter case, the service object need not be part of the same organization as the service provider. Some examples of service relationships are: (1) an accounting department in a manufacturing company, (2) a computer support person in an academic department, (3) a consulting group that provides business services to external customers, (4) an IT department that serves several business units in the same organization, and of course, (5) a service professional serving several clients.

There are at least three different types of service arrangements:

Type I: The service provider delivers services to only one service object.

Type II: The service provider delivers services to more than one service object in the same organization.

Type III: The service provider delivers services to one or more service objects in external organizations.

Once a provider type is identified, in a particular instance, the next step is to determine who pays for the service and specifically how that support is organized. This process is known as *service provisioning*.

The internal processes of effective service management go through a cyclic process, known as the *service lifecycle* that includes service strategy, service design, service transition, service operation, and continual service improvement. The use of the methodology presented in this chapter is regarded as a *best practice*. Most service organizations and all IT organizations would perform better if they adopted a set of best practices, and clearly, many of them do.

## Service as a Business

The notion of service has its origin in ancient times and was understood to mean "one person doing something for another." With the advent of civilization and industrialization, the definition of service was implicitly extended to encompass "one person doing something for an organization," usually in the form of employment. At this stage, specialization and entrepreneurship kicked in with all of their rights and privileges resulting in what we now recognize as a service organization.

Specialization has its roots in process efficiency, but has definite social overtones. Some jobs are more lucrative and have more prestige, and, for a variety of reasons, people can do some tasks better than others. Specialization is not limited to individuals but applies to organizations and groups within organizations, as well. Specialization is commonplace, not only in service organizations. In conventional business processes, such as a sales group, certain tasks are performed more expeditiously by a single individual or group, as with credit checking, when the task is performed repeatedly. The degree of specialization needed in a service process is related to the amount of repeatability. Most production and service chains divide the process into individual tasks that are performed by a single unit, taken here to be a person, group, or machine, such that efficiency and effectiveness is achieved through specialization.

Innovation flourishes in a receptive service environment, so that effective service groups are commonly at odds with their parent organization. Service spin offs have resulted in a thriving service economy through entrepreneurship and innovation.

Accordingly, it is important to recognize that *service is a business*, and that the principles given here apply equally well to internal and external service organizations.

## Service Componentization

Services are ubiquitous, so practically everyone knows what a service is. Well, maybe they can't exactly define it, but they recognize one when they see or experience it. What most people don't think about, unless they have to, is that a service is definitely a process. Beneath the surface, there is usually a collection of activities to support that process. The activities are organized into components.

A *component* is an organizational entity for instantiating services. Some components provide more than one service and some services are comprised of more that one component. The operation of a simple restaurant is used to clarify the concept of componentization.

> We go to a restaurant for a meal. The meal is the service we are seeking. We grab a table, look at the menu, and give our order to a waiter or waitress. Subsequently, the meal is delivered. We consume the meal, pay the tab, and leave. In our interaction with the waiter or waitress, we exchange information, so in a very general sense, we co-produce the service event, although we usually do not experience the meal preparation. This is not a pure service, since the food is a product. However, the service part of the meal is a service.

> On the other hand, we all know that the restaurant is a collection of interacting components that provide a meal service to one or more guests. The components of the restaurant are the server (i.e., the waiter or waitress), the kitchen (that

prepares the food), a cleaning component, a food-ordering component, an accounting component, a facility-management component, and a restaurant management component that orchestrates the services supplied by the components. The *service orchestration*, which is an explicit or implicit specification of the interactions between components, is a necessary element in the design of a managed service system.

Collectively, the arrangements of components that make up a service offering constitute its architecture. In service architecture, some components are internal persons or units, some components are outsourced, and some components are business partners. One aspect of service management is the choreography of components in a particular business process – that is, how information is passed between components without explicit direction.

Another important aspect of service management is keeping track of the components and their attributes. When a service organizations gets complicated, a service repository is required to keep track of the services that are provided by each component and what components are needed for a particular service process. Usually, a computer database is used. From a strategic viewpoint, a component is an asset that must be managed just as any other asset.

### IT Services Sourcing

There are several aspects of IT services that can vary between organizations. Examples are commonplace: computer operations, network management, hardware and software acquisition, system analysis and design, software design, software development, information systems integration, and a call center and help desk operation and management. This is a representative set of tasks necessary for sustaining an IT services organization. You can do them yourself; you can have another business entity help you do them; or you can have a business entity do them for you. In the latter two cases, the business process is known as *IT service outsourcing*.

Most IT services reflect an underlying set of IT assets, such as hardware, software, users, and systems. The IT services organization has three possible roles regarding these assets: develop or acquire, operate, and manage. For each of the IT assets, role adoption can differ. For example, hardware can be acquired internally and operated by an outside contractor.

The entity that provides the service, that is, the external business unit, need not be an independent business entity in a foreign country. It can be a separate business unit in the same enterprise, located locally, in the same country, or offshore. Alternately, it can be an independent professional services business entity in the same country – a service usually regarded as *IT consulting*. In many cases, however, the organization providing the outsourced service *is*, in fact, an independent business entity operating out of and located in a foreign country.

## *IT Services Management*

It would seem that a person's view of IT services management would be different, depending on whether your organization is the service provider or the service client, and indeed, it is. The common denominator between the various perspectives is the set of common issues that business and IT managers have to deal with, some of which are strategic planning, IT and business alignment, measurement and analysis, costs and investment, business partners and relationships, sourcing, continuous improvement, and governance. The issues are repetitive, recurring, and ongoing, and constitute a *service lifecycle*. The elements of the lifecycle are generic and do not necessarily apply to all service systems. Differences lie in the adoption and deployment of the lifecycle elements.

At the heart of IT services management is a set of tasks that involve "keeping track of things," and there are a lot of things to keep track of. We will call them *service elements*. Some of the service elements are obvious, such as users, hardware, software, network components, office facilities, and configurations. There are other service elements, mostly related to enterprise operations that can offer a challenge, such as categorization of services, to whom those services are supplied or alternately, from whom those services are obtained, contractors, outsourced projects, outsourcers, and business partners. A *service directory* is needed for this type of record keeping. Lastly, with regard to business alignment and service operations, there is a whole host of service operational elements that collectively possess business value that should not be ignored. Three of many such service operational elements are incident management, problem management, and change management. It is through the integration of service operational elements that an enterprise can achieve significant business value. The subject is covered in a later section in this chapter.

## Elements in the Service Lifecycle

The service lifecycle consists of five important elements, listed as follows: service strategy, service design, service transition, service operation, and continuous improvement. A waterfall model is usually used to suggest how the requirements process goes from strategy to continuous improvement while implementing a feedback cycle, as required. Each element of the service lifecycle is considered separately.

## *Service Strategy*

The first and most important element in the service lifecycle is service strategy. Successful service operations are not sustainable over long periods, because of environmental turbulence affecting resources, competition, and requirements. Accordingly, a service strategy is needed. A *strategy* is a long term plan, based on objectives, that allows an organization to adapt to changing conditions.

Since service is a client based endeavor, it is necessary that a service deliver perceptible value. A service strategy based on client needs is necessary for successful service operations. A service strategy, recorded in a *strategy document*, should reflect whether the strategy is intended for a provider or a client.

How an organization uses a service strategy is an individual matter. A service document should reflect major items, such as whether services are managed internally or outsourced, who the key collaborators are, and what service management functions, such as problem and incident management functions, are needed.

## *Service Design*

Service design refers to the synthesis of services to satisfy enterprise objectives. This stage has general applicability, even though it appears, on the surface to reflect specific IT services. Service design incorporates the service architecture, processes, policies, and requisite documentation. Even though the service strategy identifies various services, the service design phase is where they are established to satisfy business objectives. Even though a computer-based service is implemented offshore, it is usually conceptualized by the parent organization during this phase. Risks, quality, measurement, and infrastructure requirements are specified in this stage. Also, this stage involves capacity management, availability management, security management, and key organizational responsibilities.

### Service Transition

Service transition concerns the implementation of services in the sense of putting them into a production environment. As such, service transition is an organizational bridge between the design and the operations stages. In many instances, the service transition phase involves a change to existing services involving limited functionality and operational procedures. As such, a service transition requires the establishing of or adhering to a formal policy for the implementation of required changes and the development of a framework for the integration of the changes. When additional training and help desk support is needed, it is established in the service transition stage, which may also include system validation and testing.

## Service Operation

The function of the service operation stage is to manage and deliver the services established in the design stage. Business value to the enterprise is delivered in the operation phase, and event monitoring is of prime importance. A *service event* is a change of state during the delivery of a service that requires attention, such as an unplanned interruption of service. Two service management functions are commonly involved: incident management and problem management. *Incident management* is primarily concerned with resolving the situation and getting the system back up and running. *Problem management* focuses on determining the root cause of an event and interfaces with change management to insure that the problem is not a recurrent event.

### Continuous Improvement

Continuous improvement, or more properly, *continuous service improvement*, refers to the process of maintaining value to the enterprise of a service or set of services. Practically all service enterprises engage in continuous improvement to some degree, to protect their investment. The output of continuous improvement protocol, known as *service reporting*, feeds back into the other four stages, on an as needed basis, constituting the service lifecycle.

This stage consists of seven steps, listed as follows:

1. Define what you should measure
2. Define what you can measure
3. Gather the data
4. Process the data
5. Analyze the data
6. Report the information
7. Implement corrective action

Continuous improvement is an excellent management objective, as it suggests a means of prioritizing ongoing strategy and design activities.

### Constraint Management

A management approach to improving the operation of a manufacturing process or a service system, either of which is constrained from operating at presupposed efficiency, is known as the "Theory of Constraints," an operational methodology developed by Eliyahu Goldratt. It is related to the efficiency of value nets and pull models.

The philosophy of constraint management is exceedingly simple: find the constraint, also known as the *bottleneck*, in a process or system and fix it. Once the bottleneck is resolved, throughput will improve. In a service system, a bottleneck can prevent a service from being functional, so that constraint management may be necessary for service provisioning. Clearly, services are labor intensive, so that in the consulting or health care businesses, for example, you can't do the work if you don't have the people. Later, we will discuss the virtual workforce, which is an approach to service provisioning.

There is no need to improve every step in a process or system, because that could result in additional problems – such as the buildup of partially-completed inventory at intermediate stages. As soon as the bottleneck is identified and managed successfully, the constraint resolution scenario is repeated. The process would ordinarily continue until the law of diminishing returns kicks in. A constraint may be internal or external to the process or system under evaluation.

The process of constraint management is as straightforward as the concept itself and consists of five easy steps:

1. Identify the constraint.
2. Decide how to resolve the constraint by focusing on the functions that the constraint is supposed to perform. The constraint should not be resolved by adding tasks that the constraint is not intended to do in the first place. On the other hand, a constraint could be resolved by considering related steps in the process or system.
3. Align the functioning of other elements to the identified constraint.
4. Resolve the conflict by off-loading work from that constraint or increasing its capacity.
5. After a constraint is overcome, return to step 1 to identify additional constraints.

The constraint management process is concerned with the goals of the organization and whatever elements in the service production process that prevent achievement of those goals.

## Bottlenecks

A *bottleneck* is a work center that limits production or service. Bottlenecks occur in systems designed to be well balanced, because operating conditions and workloads customarily change over time in response to external conditions. Everyday examples of systems that develop bottlenecks are hospitals, restaurants, banks, factories, and consulting organizations. An operations or service manager usually deals with a bottleneck by increasing the capacity of the work center causing the constraint or by adjusting the operating procedures or process routing.

In the service community, especially with consulting, bottlenecks can easily occur because of a lack of people with requisite knowledge, skills, and experience. Use of a virtual workforce is a common solution to a service bottleneck.

## Virtual Workforce

A *virtual workforce* is a collection of service individuals with similar primary skills supplemented by diverse secondary skills that widen the capability of the total group. In many cases, an associate's secondary skill is just as relevant as his or her primary skill. This is commonly the case in consulting organizations where the on-demand service workload is heterogeneous, non-repeatable, and unpredictable.

## Value Nets

A *value net* is a means of capturing business value from the integration of strategy, process, workforce, and technology. Business value is created by shifting from the traditional value-chain model to the value-net model in service systems. Constraint management is applicable to value nets.

In the value-chain model, an organization creates value by adding elements to the finished product at each stage of a production process. In a general sense, raw materials are converted to value in a step-by-step production line. In the modern competitive environment, a value net provides a faster turnaround time and more operational choices, especially with regard to a service environment.

Successful enterprises currently use value nets in which suppliers and business partners interoperate through information over networks on a demand basis. The relationships between organization, suppliers, business partners, and customers are dynamic and adjust to changing requirements. Value nets are efficient because of the real time combination of services supplied by the key participants – the business, buyers, suppliers, and business partners.

### The Pull Model for Service Agility

Hagel and Brown (2007) have identified the pull model as a means of mobilizing business resources for the upcoming generation of business activities based on mass communications and the Internet. The characteristics of the *pull model* are succinctly summarized in the following sentence from the Hagel/Brown web report. "Rather than 'push,' this new approach focuses on 'pull' – creating platforms that help people to mobilize appropriate resources when the need arises." Push models are "script oriented" and thrive in stable environments with little uncertainty. Forecasting, as in demand forecasting, is key in push environments and allow high levels of efficiency to be developed in business processes. Pull models are more amenable to uncertain business conditions that require compressed development times for new goods and services.

Pull models increase value creation for both clients and providers. For clients, pull platforms expand the scope of available resources. For providers, pull platforms enhance the market for their services. In this instance, the term "platform" is intended to imply a framework for providing resources for accommodating service requirements. Pull platforms are associated with the following attributes: uncertain demand, emergent design, decentralized environment, loosely coupled modular construction, and on-demand service provisioning.

The pull model represents service architecture at the enterprise level, and could properly be viewed as a form of *enterprise service architecture.*

## Service Quality

Service quality is an involved arrangement of client expectations, client education, business value, and business utility. It is elusive because clients usually cannot assess quality until after a service event has been completed, and this is a major difference between products and services. Service providers present quality as adherence to standard operating procedures. Service clients view service quality based on expectations and value creation

In manufacturing, quality particulars are observable and quality is easily determined before the client gets involved. In services, quality turns out to be a social construct dependent upon real or perceived values. With a service, a quality assessment is instantaneously being made at each step in the service delivery process, including appointment and scheduling, service delivery, conclusion, termination, billing, and archiving.

### Client's View of Service Quality

Service quality is determined by a client's expectation of service and the client's perception of the service that is experienced. Expectations are developed by word of mouth, personal needs, and past experience. The service that is delivered is a complex combination of reliability, responsiveness, assurance, empathy, and tangibles. *Reliability* refers to the consistency of service. *Responsiveness* reflects the perception that the provider is willing to provide service. *Assurance* is a measure of the competence of the service provider. *Empathy* is a reflection of the personal attention afforded to clients. The area known as *Tangibles* refers to the infrastructure as it is related to the service experience. Certainly, the five attributes of service quality reflect a traditional setting and do not take into account the complications associated with technology driven service provisioning.

### Process View of Service Quality

*A service is a process.* This notion is paramount to recognizing the far-reaching importance of service systems as an academic discipline. A service takes input and produces output. In between the input and the output, there exist one or more steps that constitute the service process. Consider a simple medical example. A patient – the client – perceives a situation that requires attention. A contact with a medical provider is made and an appointment is scheduled for a service event. In general, the following three items of information are brought to the service process: the patient per se, a medical history, and the relevant information for the current problem. This is the client/customer input required for a service process. The physician performs the requisite consultation, diagnosis, and resolution that collectively constitute the service process. The output then consists of the diagnosis, prescription, prognosis, and update of the medical records. Additionally, the personal knowledge bases of the patient and physician are enhanced as a result of the service event. The quality issue stems from the fact that the provider and the client view the service process from differing points of view. Service organizations tend to regard the input-process-output model as a functional entity comprised of individual steps and the client views the process as an end-to–end sequence of operations.

### *Enterprise View of Quality*

At the enterprise level, service quality is a function of the value proposition for the client, so that in a real sense

Quality = Value

where a service supports business objectives and focuses on business value. The key determinants of business value are transaction costs, usually delineated as follows:

- Overall costs of exchange between two parties
- Finding and selecting suppliers of services
- Negotiating agreements
- Costs of consuming services
- Governing the relationship with suppliers
- Ensuring that commitments are fulfilled

In this book, we recommend a value proposition based on utility and warranty. *Utility* is derived by the client from the characteristics of the service that have a positive effect on the performance of requisite tasks. *Warranty* is derived from the recognition of positive outcomes when provided in needed capacity, continuity, and reliability. *Warranty is what the customer gets and utility is how it is delivered.*

## Utility Computing

Every year, businesses spend millions of dollars on their IT infrastructure consisting of hardware, system software, applications, networks, people, and other organizational assets. With "on demand" computing, they can plug into the wall, figuratively, speaking, and only pay for the IT services they use. The concept is called *utility computing* that is accessed as are most public utilities. We are going to denote the utility computing concept as *E-Services.* An E-Service utility is a viable option for obtaining computing services.

The concept of E-Services in the packaging of computer services is a metered facility without up-front costs for IT infrastructure and is commonly used for large-scale computations or peak demands. In the current view of things, an E-Services utility is network based and is dependent upon the Internet as a transport mechanism. In recent years, computing has become the operational medium for business, government, and education and part of everyday life for most people. As with electric utilities, computing utilities have evolved from being a luxury to an everyday necessity.

An E-Service utility is characterized by four key factors: necessity, reliability, usability, and scalability. *Necessity* refers to the idea that a preponderance of users depend on the utility to satisfy everyday needs. *Reliability* refers to the expectation that the utility will be available when the user requires it. *Usability* refers to the requirement that the utility is easy and convenient to use – regardless of the complexity of the underlying infrastructure. *Scalability* refers to the fact that the utility has sufficient capacity to allow the users to experience the benefits of an expandable utility that provides economy of scale. Certainly, modern Internet facilities for search operations that engage thousands of servers satisfy these characteristics.

The notion of "paying for what one uses" is a compelling argument for using E-Services for special or all computing needs. However, the proof of the pudding may in fact be in the details. The key question is whether the service should be based on a metered model or a subscription model. With the *metered model*, the usage is easily measured, monitored, and verified and lends itself to managerial control on the part of the user. In addition, metering can be applied to differing levels of service. With the *subscription model,* usage is difficult to control and monitor, and its adoption is favored by mangers more concerned with convenience than with resource control.

For example, water and electricity service commonly use metered service while the plain ordinarily telephone system "usually" provides subscription service for local service and metered service for long distance. In the area of computer networks, broadband cable and telephone digital-subscriber line (DSL) rates are normally based on the subscription model. With cable TV, on the other hand, there are usually differing levels of subscription service along with "pay per view" for special services.

One can readily conceptualize a scheme for a typical E-Service customer – nominally assumed to be a small-to-medium-sized business. Office services, such as word and spreadsheet processing, could be subscription-based service and special applications, such as integrated enterprise systems, would be metered service.

The difference between application services and multi-tenant services may very well be the deciding factor in determining whether metered or subscriber service is the way to go. With *multi-tenant service,* several clients may share the same software with separate data – as in the case of office processing. With *application service,* the service provider supplies one instance of the software per client, thereby lending itself to a form of metered service.

## Quick Summary

1. There are three forces operating in the sphere of service processes. The first is the use of ICT as an enabler in providing revenue growth, efficiency, and effectiveness for traditional and enhanced services, as well as for conventional business processes. This subject is commonly referred to as information systems. The second is the consulting services domain that provides IT services to external organizations.

The third is the use of ICT to manage information systems and services, which is a field of endeavor known as IT Services Management.

2. The notion of service has its origin in ancient times and was understood to mean "one person doing something for another." With the advent of civilization and industrialization, the definition of service was implicitly extended to encompass "one person doing something for an organization," usually in the form of employment. At this stage, specialization and entrepreneurship kicked in with all of their rights and privileges resulting in what we now recognize as the service organization.

3. Information is a critical asset in the operation of an enterprise and in the everyday lives of individuals. In a figurative sense, information is the grease that allows the components to work together. IT is employed to handle the information needed to manage the operations of an enterprise and to aid in making effective decisions. Thus, IT is a service to the enterprise, regardless if that enterprise is concerned with production processes, service operations, government reporting, professional services, scientific services, technical services, or personal services.

4. There are several aspects of IT services that can vary between organizations. Examples are commonplace: computer operations, network management, hardware and software acquisition, system analysis and design, software design, software development, information systems integration, and call center and help desk operation and management. This is a representative set of tasks necessary for sustaining an IT services organization. You can do them yourself; you can have another business entity help you do them; or you can have a business entity do them for you. In the latter two cases, the business process is known as *IT service outsourcing.*

5. The service lifecycle consists of five important elements, listed as follows: service strategy, service design, service transition, service operation, and continuous improvement.

6. A management approach to improving the operation of a manufacturing process or a service system, either of which is constrained from operating at presupposed efficiency, is known as the "Theory of Constraints." The philosophy of constraint management is exceedingly simple: find the constraint, also known as the *bottleneck*, in a process or system and fix it. Once the bottleneck is resolved, throughput will improve. In a service system, a bottleneck can prevent a service from being functional, so that constraint management may be necessary for service provisioning. Clearly, services are labor intensive, so that in the consulting or health care businesses, for example, you can't do the work if you don't have the people.

7. Service quality is a complex arrangement of client expectations, client education, business value, and business utility. It is elusive because clients usually cannot assess quality until after a service event has been completed. Service providers present quality as adherence to standard operating procedures. Service clients view service quality based on expectations and value creation

8. Every year, businesses spend millions of dollars on their IT infrastructure consisting of hardware, system software, applications, networks, people, and other organizational assets. With "on demand" computing, they can plug into the wall, figuratively speaking, and only pay for the IT services they use. The concept is called *utility computing* that is accessed as most public utilities. The utility computing concept is known as *E-Services*.

## Key Terms

The reader should be familiar with the following terms in the context in which they were used in the chapter.

| | |
|---|---|
| Bottleneck | Service directory |
| Business unit | Service element |
| Constraint | Service lifecycle |
| Constraint management | Service object |
| Consulting domain | Service operation |
| Continual service improvement | Service orchestration |
| Information system | Service provider |
| IT service outsourcing | Service quality |
| IT services management | Service strategy |
| Pull model | Service transition |
| Push model | Types of service arrangement |
| Service component | Value net |
| Service design | Virtual workforce |

## Selected Reading

Cherbakov, L., et al, (2005). "Impact of service orientation at the business level", *IBM Systems Journal*, Vol. 44, No. 4.

Fitzsimmons, J. and Fitzsimmons, M. (2008). *Service Management: Operations, Strategy, Information Technology* (6th Edition), New York: McGraw-Hill/Irwin.

Ganek, A. and Kloeckner, K. (2007). "An overview of IBM Service Management," *IBM Systems Journal*, Vol. 46, No. 3.

Hagel, J. and Brown, J. (2007). *From Push to Pull: Emerging Models for Mobilizing Resources,* www.edgeperspectives.com.

Heizer, J. and Render, B. (2006). *Operations Management* (8ᵗʰ Edition), Upper Saddle River, NJ: Pearson Prentice-Hall.

Hurwitz, J., Bloor, R., Baroudi, C., and Kaufman, M. (2007). *Service Oriented Architecture for Dummies,* Hoboken, NJ: Wiley Publishing, Inc.

ITIL. (2007). *Service Strategy,* London: The Stationary Office.

Metters, R., King-Metters, K., Pullman, M., and Walton, S. (2006). *Successful Service Operations Management* (2e), Boston: Thomson Course Technology.

Nichols, M. (2007). "Quality Tools in a Service Environment," www.ASQ.org.

Rappa, M. (2004). "The utility business model and the future of computing services," *IBM Systems Journal*, Vol. 43, No. 1.

.Ricketts, J. (2008). *Reaching the Goal: How Managers Improve a Services Business Using Goldratt's Theory of Constraints,* Upper Saddle River, NJ: IBM Press/Pearson plc.

# 5

---

# SERVICE BUSINESS

A worldwide service economy has emerged through globalization and digitization. As a direct result, the modern enterprise has an operational border based on a portfolio of services obtained through make, buy, or rent decisions. The decisions are taken, of course, through an analysis of transaction costs. This flexibility has been fueled by service design, service innovation, service marketing, and Internet-based business models. In the latter case, inexpensive and wide-spread computing and interoperability have practically eliminated geographic barriers to growth and flexibility. This chapter describes a business model based on services.

## Service Business Concepts

Several important factors have contributed to a business model based on services. The complexity of the modern work environment is perhaps the key factor as well as the changing demands of a networked economy. The increased level of worldwide incomes has added to the desire for enhanced business and social services. The dependence on information and communications technology (ICT) has been an enabler of the complexity and growth of services by facilitating the connection between suppliers and consumers of services.

### *Business Model*

A *business model* for services is a representation of a business emphasizing its purpose, strategies, organization and operational practices, and capabilities. It typically covers the following: core capabilities, partner network, value proposition, customer base, distribution methods, cost structure, and revenue base. The main function of a business's organization and operational structures is to translate the business model into an objective reality.

The point of view taken here is that an operational service model is a valid form of business model.

### *Strategy and Mission*

A *strategy* is defined as "A long term plan of action designed to achieve a particular goal," and *governance* is defined as "The set of processes, customs, policies, laws, and institutions affecting the way an endeavor is directed, administered, or controlled." The two subjects command our attention, because much of the economy and workforce are engaged in services; but, as we have alluded to before, we seem to know the least about what we do the most.

The basic tenet underlying strategy is that a principal entity desires to accomplish something worthwhile generally known as the *mission*. A mission is required so the entity, be it a business, firm, government agency, educational unit, or person, knows where it is going, and a strategy is needed so it knows how to get there. The mission is a service participant's goal, and the strategy is the roadmap for achieving that goal. A *strategy* is a plan of action.

### *Service Ecosystem*

Before the revolution in ICT services, the exchange of information was a supporting element in most aspects of economic activity. Through advanced technology, information is now an important component in the value proposition of most enterprises.

The modern enterprise can now exploit informational resources on a demand basis from remote locations and without necessarily owning them. Those resources exist as a service to the enterprise. Moreover, the facilities necessary to sustain those resources may be shared, creating innovative opportunities for service provisioning.

Through web sites, mobile computing, and kiosks, self-service channels are currently available to support informational interchange. Business functions, such as billing, payments, ordering and order processing, reservations, online service support, and information management are currently available without regard to time or distance.

Through innovation and entrepreneurship, new business opportunities are available on an on-demand basis, frequently constructed from existing services.

### Strategic Assets

A *strategic asset* is a resource that provides the basis for one or more core competencies, economic benefit, and competitive advantage, thereby enabling a service business to provide distinctive service in the marketplace. Because services are labor intensive, investments in people, processes, knowledge, and infrastructure are directly analogous to investments in resources for production and distribution in capital intensive businesses.

Strategic assets permit a service enterprise to achieve a competitive advantage through service differentiation, cost advantage, and superior customer response. *Service differentiation* involves providing a high degree of uniqueness in the service experience and also in the quality of service provided. *Cost advantage* refers to efficiency in the use of facilities, as in an airline terminal, and with 24/7 operations to maximize the use of infrastructure. *Customer response* involves flexible, reliable, and timely solutions to customer requirements.

### Service Context

A *service context* supports the efficacy of service provisioning. The development of a service context involves the asking of tough questions to examine the strategic goal and objectives of a service organization in order to identify and establish a service portfolio. Here are some questions a service organization might want to ask of itself:

- What services should we offer?
- To whom should the services be offered?
- How do we achieve competitive advantage?
- What is our customer's value proposition?
- How do we establish value for our stakeholders?
- How do we define service quality?
- How do we allocate strategic assets to our service portfolios?
- What are the bottlenecks to growth and effective service provisioning (i.e., constraint management)?

The questions apply in differing degrees to whether services are provisioned for one organization (or department), one of more units within the same parent organization, or to units in different organizations. Moreover, service applies within the following contexts: do it yourself, have another business entity help you do it, and have another business entity do it for you.

### Service Perspective

Every reasonable business model demands a context, and the one that we present in this chapter is no exception. Our service model is based on a service management concept for providing value to customers in the form of capabilities that translate resources into valuable services.

The objective of service provisioning – regardless of whether the service involves people processing, possession processing, or information processing – is to provide value to customers through an intrinsic knowledge of customer needs obtained by preparation, analysis, usage patterns, and the application of best practices. Within this perspective, a *service* may be alternately defined as a means of delivering value to customers by facilitating outcomes customers want to achieve without the ownership of specific costs and risks.

### Service Systems Thinking

The objective of a service business is to assist in making resources available to the client as services, and in the process, creating value for both provider and client. This is a worthwhile objective, to be sure, but some basic questions must first be answered. Who are the client and the provider? What are the resources? What geopolitical forces are involved? Does the nature of the service itself play an important role in the process of value creation? However, a very basic question is yet to be asked. Are we service creationists or are we service evolutionists? The answer to this particular question will determine precisely how we approach the subject matter. Before we get going with the discussion of the subject, one of the questions can be answered right off the top, and it has to do with resources. For any organization we are going to consider, the key resources are people, organization, infrastructure, technology, and capital. All service businesses are resource intensive and success is directly the result of the level of resources that he entrepreneur can apply to the situation.

## Service Factors

Three factors determine the need for services and the realization of those services. They are: value, flexibility and control, and risk. With regard to the value factor, it is not just value, per se, but value versus cost. When costs are reduced through internal or external outsourcing, for example, there is a normal concern over whether the value to the client is the same as or greater than before the outsourcing. Using resources and capability as inputs to an analysis of a service, the key question concerns the resultant value to the client considering the cost. Similarly, when internal or external outsourcing is implemented, there is concern over operational flexibility and management control. Some organizations have experienced the "tail wagging the dog" syndrome and have had to bring major service, such as IT outsourcing, back into the parent organization. It is very difficult to modify strong service level agreements once they are established, so the parent organization is effectively constrained by the very services that were supposed to provide them with business agility. Also, successful outsourcing, in some instances, has effectively been jeopardized through mergers and acquisition, whereby competing services have been assimilated into a parent organization thereby comprising the original benefits. Lastly, there is risk inherent in relying on services, although there is a customary risk in everyday affairs. The uncertainty in the application of service level agreements works contrary to the expectation on the part of clients to receive a positive effect with the utilization of assets. To inject a bit of reality into the analysis, there is always the headache factor. The possibility always exists that outsourcing or calling in a consultant, is a means of getting rid of an organizational or operational headache – regardless of the cost.

## Provider-Side View of Service Provisioning

In most views of service theory, there would appear to be service creationist forces at work. Through some unknown process, an enterprise comes to life and ostensibly needs service of some kind. A service organization enters the scene and identifies certain processes associated with the enterprise that it can use to make a profit. At least, this is the manner in which some service providers look at it. It's clear that the target enterprise is the service client, and the service organization is the service provider. The activity on the part of the provider that identifies candidate processes for the proposed benefit of the client is sometimes called *service innovation*. Usually, service innovation amounts to very little more than an elementary form of observational research. In general, however, the tasks involved with creating and sustaining a service business usually constitute a rational process. The provider may possess superior capability, as is commonly the case with an IT consulting company that provides a variety of services to less experienced clients who choose to take advantage of the opportunity. The client's resources may be inadequate to effectively perform a particular set of tasks, as in the case of an enterprise that doesn't possess the needed people or technology to solve a particular problem or venture into a new area of endeavor. The client, in either of the cases, may choose to focus on core competency. In this instance, a core competency is a set of activities that affect the mission of the client. The use of services may be purely economic, which is usually the basis for most outsourcing.

Service creationism represents a provider–side view of service provisioning.

## Client-Side View of Service Provisioning

On the other hand, a service evolutionist might view the subject of service provisioning in a different manner. With client-side service provisioning, the process of obtaining and deploying services evolves through several identifiable stages of organizational dynamics, based on the three factors presented above, namely value, flexibility, and risk.

Most enterprise processes are comprised of two kinds of activities: core functionality and supporting functionality. In a bank loan department, for example, the lending function is core, and credit checking is supporting. Similarly, in a pension writing department, the synthesis of a pension plan is core, and the back-office computer operations are supplementary. When multiple departments demand the same services, it is a common management decision to combine the service operations and, in the process, possibly enhance the level of service. "Kick it up a notch" is the usual justification. This is the first stage, referred to here as the *service recognition stage*.

At this point the emphasis changes from operating a service to using a service on the part of the core departments. The core department is avoiding the risks and costs associated with the supplementary function, since service costs are shared. Let us call this the *risk/cost avoidance* stage.

After the need for non-core services is realized and instantiated, there is a universal tendency to reduce costs – because after all, the services are not core to the mission of the organization – or endeavor to make a profit on the service operation. A decision can be taken at this point to spin off the service department as a self-standing internal or external organization, or outsource the total operation to an outside service firm. It would appear that this is either the *spin off stage* or the *outsource stage*, as the case may be.

There are additional considerations, based on infrastructure and management control. Here are some options:

- Outsource the total operation, including infrastructure, people, and management control
- Retain infrastructure and management control and outsource the people and operations

- Retain infrastructure, management control, and operations and outsource the people
- Outsource certain tasks within any of the above options

*Task-oriented outsourcing* is perhaps the end-game in the relationship between enterprise dynamics and service environment. It is commonplace in modern business to have professional and technical tasks, such as engineering, software development, and design outsourced to specialist firms in much the same way that architectural services have existed for many years.

### Business Value Creation

A *service business* is a collection of organizational assets that provide value to clients in the form of services by exploiting inherent capability on two levels: the client level and the provider level. Effective service provisioning permits the client to focus on core competencies.

The value of a service is determined by a client's expectation of service and the client's perception of the service that is experienced. Expectations are developed by word of mouth, personal needs, and past experience. The service that is delivered is a complex combination of five attributes: reliability, responsiveness, assurance, empathy, and tangibles. *Reliability* refers to the consistency of service. *Responsiveness* reflects the perception that the provider is willing to provide service. *Assurance* is a measure of the competence of the service provider. *Empathy* is a reflection of the personal attention afforded to clients. *Tangibles* refer to the infrastructure as it is related to the service experience. The five attributes of service quality reflect a traditional setting and do not take into account the complications associated with technology driven service provisioning.

To this important list, it seems important to add availability, capacity, continuity, and security.

## Availability, Capacity, Continuity, Security, and Risk

*Availability* reflects the degree to which services are available for use by clients under terms and conditions agreed upon in a service-level agreement. Clearly, a service is available only if the client can take advantage of it. Accessibility and expectations are major considerations from the user's perspective. The method of access should be made explicit in the service-level agreement and the user's expectations should be managed by the client.[1]

*Capacity* is the ability of the service and the service provider to support the requisite level of business activity of the client. Demand for service must be availability within a specified range and the service provider must be able to supply service provisioning during peak periods in a shared environment.

*Continuity* refers to the ability on the part of the service provider to support capacity during disruptive and catastrophic events. Continued service is not the only consideration. Alternate and backup facilities in the form of services must be in the service landscape.

*Security* refers to controls to assure that client assets will be safe from intrusion, disclosure, and physical safety. Security refers to operational security *and* to the physical safeguard of client assets.

Availability, capacity, continuity, and security collectively determine the client's risk in acquiring services and differentiating between service providers. When comparing the cost and value of services, risk should always be factored into the equation.

## Service Assets

Engaging in a business service would appear to be quite straightforward on the surface but is actually a complex arrangement of business units, service units, services that connect the two, and provider types. The abstract term *business unit* refers to the provider assets that give value to the client when applied. Similarly, *service asset* refers to the functions that the provider can perform. It follows that a *business service* is a mapping between the provider and the client, in much the same way that we ordinarily conceptualize the physician/patient relationship.

## *Service Portfolio*

A *service portfolio* is a conceptual collection or list of services. Use of the term is intended to be analogous to a financial portfolio of investment instruments. However, there are major differences depending upon the reason for the development of the portfolio.

A financial portfolio is ordinarily thought to be a collection of assets synthesized so that when the value of one asset goes down, another goes up. This is a bit of a simplification, but it's the idea that counts. The best case is when the value of the assets goes up, and the worst case is when the value of the assets goes down. Normal life is somewhere in between. With a service portfolio, there should never be a downside, but some service firms do some things better than others.

With services, the conceptualization of the portfolio depends on whether you are talking to a provider or a client. A provider portfolio might be a simple list of services – something an accounting firm might have as part of their marketing collateral. Similarly, an IT consulting business, for example, could list items such as strategy formulation, service programming, and operations management.

From the client perspective, however, a service portfolio is indispensable, because it provides a central source of services agreed to in conjunction with the service provider, along with terms, conditions, and service metrics. A related concern is a database of potential suppliers of services. A comprehensive service needs portfolio often results in an effective service-level agreement.

## Service-Level Management

A service-level agreement (SLA) is a formal and signed agreement between the service provider organization and the business unit to document expectations and requirements of a service delivered to the business unit from the service provider. The agreement aligns business needs with delivery of services and facilitates delivery of solutions to business requirements at acceptable cost. It involves a definition of requirements, an agreement on specifications, operations management expectations, and a review clause. The tasks include the creation of a service catalog, the development of internal procedures, the ability to monitor and respond to operational conditions, and the ability to perform regular service-level reviews. The service catalog delineates the priority of service-level tasks, the expected effect on employees, a description of users, a listing and description of service assets, and the organization's business partners and suppliers. Service-level monitoring is a key issue. The major service metrics are availability, responsiveness, performance, integrity and accuracy, and security incidents. In order to perform the service-level monitoring, the following steps are required: the identification and criteria for monitoring, establishing thresholds, the definition of alert, the specification of alert management, and essential response definition.

Service-level determination and management is the key element in a service package.

## Availability Management

*Availability management* is the service management function that insures that a given service consistently and effectively delivers the level of support required by the customer. Continuity of service is the key objective. The usual risks to availability relate to technology, business processes, operational procedures, and human error. Countermeasures that have proven to enhance availability are testing of business processes, effective release procedures, and employee training. The areas most affected by availability issues are the implementation of new IT services, critical business functions, supplier behavior, and internal organizational factors, such as policies, procedures, and tools.

### Capacity Management

*Capacity management* is the service management function that optimizes the capability of the service infrastructure and supporting organization to deliver the required level of customer service in the established time domain. Capability of service is the key objective. This element is most affected by people, infrastructure, and technology.

### Service-Desk Management

The service desk is a single point of contact for customers and service technicians with the intent of delivering responsive solutions to service needs. The major service desk functions are to handle single incidents and individual service requests. Service desk scheduling has historically been a concern and the current trend is to have self-managed teams that utilize service triads or peak period scheduling. A *triad* consists of a three person team, with two people on and one off at any time.

### Incident Management

The objective of incident management is to detect events that disrupt or prevent execution of critical or normal IT services, and to respond to those events with methods of restoring normal services as quickly as possible. An *incident* is any event that is not part of the standard operation of a business process that causes, or may cause, an interruption to, or reduction in, the quality of service. In this context, a *problem* is the root cause of an incident; a *solution* is a method for resolving an incident or problem that resolves the underlying cause; and a *workaround* is a means of restoring a specific incident without resolving the underlying cause.

## Problem Management

The objective of problem management is to investigate and analyze the root causes of incidents and initiate changes to service assets to resolve the underlying problem. The key function of problem management is to reduce the impact of incidents, problems, and errors on the organization by applying methods of root cause and trend analysis.

## Change Management

The objective of change management is to provide a formal process for introducing changes to the service environment with a minimal amount of disruption to normal service operations, while insuring the integrity of critical business functions. Change management usually goes through several distinct steps: change initiation, change request, change classification, change authorization, release management, and review by a change board.

Incident management is focused on restoring normal service and identifies resolution actions; problem management is focused on the identification and resolution of underlying problems and their root causes; and change management deploys changes developed by incident or problem management.

### Directory-Services Management

The service directory is a database of service assets. Directory services is essentially a database from which users can obtain information on service assets through a secure and organized process that is accessible through appropriate information and communications technology (ICT) facilities. The major directory service functions are to record change events, describe connectivity, track service objects, and identify assets in the service landscape.

## Governance

A typical organization has a group of stakeholders who have something to gain if the organization is successful and something to lose if the organization is not successful. The gain could be financial in nature, as in the case of investors, or qualitative in nature, as in the case of non-profit or social organizations. Success or failure is a relative assessment, as is the concept of gain or loss on the part of the stakeholders. The stakeholders, often referred to as the *principals*, give the right to manage the organization to *agents*, ostensibly qualified to do so and are rewarded accordingly, through the application of policies and rules that represent the principals' best interests. The process is generally known as governance, a word derived from the Latin verb "to steer." Agents are often high-level or middle-level managers that derive short and long-term monetary gains that are directly related to the organization's success. There are as many forms of governance as there are organizations to control. Even though the words are similar, governance does not imply local, regional, or central government.

The principles of effective *corporate governance* are well-defined and usually implemented through "boards of directors" and other forms of governing bodies. Governance is usually related to consistent management, cohesive policies, and effective decision rights.

*Information technology (IT) governance* is generally regarded as a subset of corporate governance, as it relates to the operational management of IT systems. IT governance deals primarily with the connection between business focus and IT management and often involves the organization's IT application portfolio. IT governance is an important consideration in corporate governance because of the typically large budgets for IT infrastructure.

*Service governance* is a subset of IT governance to assure the principals that the development and use of services are executed according to best practices. Two factors relate to service governance. The first factor involves the high-level of outsourcing of IT functionality. The main concern is the loss of control to an external service provider, and also the long-term loss of capability in critical areas of competence.

The second factor is in the evolution to service-oriented architecture for the development of business/enterprise applications. The synthesis of applications from components accessed over the Internet from external service providers constitutes a long-term dependency with which many principals are not comfortable. In this case, the principals may want to use service governance as a means of protecting the long-term interest and possibly the intellectual capital of the parent organization.

## Quick Summary

1. A *business model* is a representation of a business emphasizing its purpose, strategies, organization and operational practices, and capabilities. It typically covers the following: core capabilities: partner network, value proposition, customer base, distribution methods, cost structure, and revenue base.

2. A *strategy* has been defined as "A long term plan of action designed to achieve a particular goal," and *governance* as

"The set of processes, customs, policies, laws, and institutions affecting the way an endeavor is directed, administered, or controlled."

3. A *strategic asset* is a resource that provides the basis for core competencies, economic benefit, and competitive advantage, thereby enabling a service business to provide distinctive service in the marketplace. Because services are labor intensive, investments in people, processes, knowledge, and infrastructure are directly analogous to investments in resources for production and distribution in capital intensive businesses.

4. The objective of service provisioning – regardless of whether the service involves people processing, possession processing, or information processing – is to provide value to customers through an intrinsic knowledge of customer needs obtained by preparation, analysis, usage patterns, and the application of best practices. Within this perspective, a *service* may be alternately defined as a means of delivering value to customers by facilitating outcomes customers want to achieve without the ownership of specific costs and risks.

5. The objective of a service business is to assist in making resources available to the client as services, and in the process, creating value for both provider and client. The value of a service is determined by a client's expectation of service and the client's perception of the service that is experienced. Expectations are developed by word of mouth, personal needs, and past experience. The service that is delivered is a complex combination of five attributes: reliability, responsiveness, assurance, empathy, and tangibles.

6. An *operations framework* is a set of service functions established as best practices that assist in providing business value to a client.

The reader should be familiar with the following terms in the context in which they were used in the chapter.

| | |
|---|---|
| Availability | Security |
| Availability management | Service assurance |
| Business model | Service business |
| Capacity | Service control |
| Capacity management | Service-desk management |
| Change management | Service-level management |
| Continuity | Service portfolio |
| Directory management | Service reliability |
| Governance | Service responsiveness |
| Incident management | Strategic asset |
| Problem management | Strategy |
| Mission | |

## Selected Reading

Carter, S. (2007). The *New Language of Business*, Upper Saddle River, NJ: IBM Press.

Clark, J. (2007). *Everything you ever wanted to know about ITIL® in less than one thousand words! Connect Sphere Limited, www. connectsphere.com.*

Collier, D. and Evans, J. (2007). *Operations Management: Goods, Services, and Value Chains*, Mason OH: Thomson Higher Education.

Fitzsimmons, J. and Fitzsimmons, M. (2008). *Service Management: Operations, Strategy, Information Technology* (6th Edition), New York: McGraw-Hill/Irwin.

Heizer, J. and Render, B. (2006). *Operations Management* (8th Edition), Upper Saddle River, NJ: Pearson Prentice-Hall.

Hurwitz, J., Bloor, R., Baroudi, C., and Kaufman, M. (2007). *Service Oriented Architecture for Dummies*, Hoboken, NJ: Wiley Publishing, Inc.

Krafzig, D., Banke, K., and Slama, D. (2005). *Enterprise SOA: Service-Oriented Architecture Best Practices*, Upper Saddle River, NJ: Prentice Hall.

Woods, D. and Mattern, T. (2006). *Enterprise SOA: Designing IT for Business Innovation*, Sebastopol, CA: O'Reilly Media Inc.

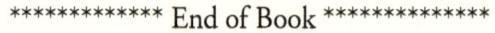

\*\*\*\*\*\*\*\*\*\*\*\*\* End of Book \*\*\*\*\*\*\*\*\*\*\*\*\*

# INDEX

ICT. See Information and Communications Technology.
Incident management 94
Information 35
Information and communications technology 22,59, 60
Information processing service 9,39
Information service xiv, 33, 45
Information system 22
Information technology 25, 60
Instant messaging 51
Intangible service xiii
Interaction service 40
Internet telephone 52
IT. See Information Technology.

Maglio, P. 19, 21
Maintenance, repair, and operations 48
Matlock, T. 18
Middleware 41
Mission 83
Mobile service facilities 18
MRO. See Maintenance, Repair, and Operations.
Multiclient service 42

Newsgroup 55

Offshoring 24
Operand information 37
Operant information 37
Orchestration 4
Ordinary mail 35